Advance Praise for *Silencing Ivan Illich Revisited*

"David Gabbard's lesson in this timeless book on Ivan Illich is that any conversation about schooling and society, especially now in our era of 'post-truth,' is both an examination of the idea of schooling itself, and, perhaps more importantly, a look into how ideas themselves circulate through systems of power."

—*Kristopher Holland, University of Cincinnati*

"Silencing Ivan Illich *Revisited* exhumes the discursive corpus of Ivan Illich and performs a unique pedagogical autopsy that begs the question of why Illich's work has not been given the same archival place as other reformation/revolutionary discourses. Gabbard delivers an Illichian critique of education and schools qua objects bound to the edificial and ideological presuppositions of the state reminiscent of Althusser. Why has Illich been so overlooked or neglected in the critical discourses of education? Gabbard explores and critiques the messianic ideology and opportunism that lead educational academics to form de facto dogmatic allegiances that reduced the discourse to a singular trajectory (i.e., messianic) in educational reform. Here is a timely provocation to abandon the "singular" for a more illuminated contemplation of an educational black hole whereby we view the event horizon and the contemplation of a "singularity" that is the possible deschooling qua education. To question education beyond the confinement of state compulsory schooling seems to have ex-communicated Illich. However, as Gabbard returns to this underlying theme of the messianic, Illich could not be ex-communicated from something that he had no membership with in the first place. In short, Silencing Ivan Illich Revisited provokes us to think about Illich in a way that we cannot ignore when it comes to the current educational ideologies that have been exclusionary to those discourses that propose a differing, even antagonistic, realm of conceptualizing schooling, school reform, and the very notion of education as a didactic human endeavor in an increasingly globalized world."

—*Antonio Garcia, Zizekian Institute*

Silencing Ivan Illich Revisited

Silencing Ivan Illich Revisited

A Foucauldian Analysis of Intellectual Exclusion

WRITTEN BY
David Gabbard

Gorham, Maine

Published by Myers Education Press, LLC
P.O. Box 424 Gorham, ME 04038

Myers Education Press is an academic publisher specializing in books, e-books and digital content in the field of education. All of our books are subjected to a rigorous peer review process and produced in compliance with the standards of the Council on Library and Information Resources.

LIBRARY OF CONGRESS CATALOGING-IN-PUBLICATION DATA AVAILABLE FROM LIBRARY OF CONGRESS.

13-digit ISBN 978-1-9755-0228-7 (paperback)
13-digit ISBN 978-1-9755-0227-0 (hard cover)
13-digit ISBN 978-1-9755-0229-4 (library networkable e-edition)
13-digit ISBN 978-1-9755-0230-0 (consumer e-edition)

Printed in the United States of America.

All first editions printed on acid-free paper that meets the American National Standards Institute Z39-48 standard.

Books published by Myers Education Press may be purchased at special quantity discount rates for groups, workshops, training organizations, and classroom usage. Please call our customer service department at 1-800-232-0223 for details.

Cover design by Sophie Appel

Visit us on the web at www.myersedpress.com to browse our complete list of titles.

Table of Contents

1. Foreword 1
2. Preface to *Revisited* 3
3. Preface (1993 Edition) 7
4. Chapter 1: To Explain an Exclusion 9
5. Chapter 2: Theoretico-Activism 17
6. Chapter 3: To Deny the Pastoral 27
7. Chapter 4: Practices of Exclusion 55
8. Chapter 5: An Analogous Exclusion 75
9. Chapter 6: The Archive and Other Transgressions 91
10. Index 113
11. About the Author 117

Foreword

MY EDITOR ONCE asked me in the 1970s, "Why are you trying to write yourself out of a job?" He was referring to my discussion of the possibility of eliminating the institution of the modern school. I had to admit it was a perplexing situation. Here I was discussing abolishing the very institution that seemed to justify my job and income as a professor of teacher education. Adding to the perplexity of my situation was the feeling that I was being ostracized by other educators who identified themselves as radical or liberal. While they were critical of many aspects of the modem school, they seemed unwilling to follow the next logical step in their critique and call for the replacement of modern school systems with some other means of education. Often, I wondered, were these radical educators unwilling to follow this line of reasoning because they would destroy the ideas that justified their jobs and income.

David Gabbard provides an answer to these unsettling questions by examining why educators had such difficulty dealing with Ivan Illich's idea of deschooling society. As David demonstrates, Illich questioned the fundamental justifications for the existence of modern school systems. While radical and liberal educators were simply critiquing the practices of modern school systems, Illich was taking the next step by arguing that the institution should not be reformed but abolished. As David argues, most educators were unable to free themselves from the assumptions that the school could save society and that the school should play a role in shaping moral and social values.

Even today, radical and liberal educators criticize school systems for not trying to save society according to their agenda and for not disseminating their values to society. They never question the right of an institution that claims to be educational to have these functions.

In a broader context, David Gabbard's book not only demonstrates why educators were unwilling to accept Illich's critique of their role as saviors of society and guardians of social values, but it is also an important contribution to our understanding of the politics of ideas. Why do some ideas have a lasting impact on society? Why do some ideas neatly fit into current discourses? Why are some ideas so radical that it might take generations before they find a comfortable common discourse? What is the role of institutions and political power in determining which ideas will gain prominence? These and other important questions are central to Gabbard's study of the silencing of Ivan Illich.

—Joel Spring
At Old Westbury, March 5, 1993

Preface to *Revisited*

SILENCING IVAN ILLICH (1993) began as a research question: considering the popularity of *Deschooling Society* in the 1970s, how can we explain the exclusion of Illich from educational discourse by the 1980s? Why had no one picked up on his ideas and carried them forward as they had with Paulo Freire's *Pedagogy of the Oppressed*, which was published (in English) the very same year (1970)? The post-structuralist writings of Michel Foucault, *The Archaeology of Knowledge* (1982) in particular, proved very beneficial in helping me to explain how, like all discourses, educational discourse is governed by particular sets of rules that determine what can and cannot be said. These rules set the boundaries of what statements and ideas will be included within a given field, and what statements and ideas will be excluded. Through my writing of *Silencing Ivan Illich*, I concluded that one rule reigns supreme over educational discourse, and it helps us explain why we have come to conflate the value of education with the institution of compulsory schooling. This rule states that in order to speak legitimately of education, in order to have your ideas included and taken seriously within educational discourse, you must present the institution of state-mandated, compulsory schooling as a benevolent institution capable of delivering the individual and/or society into some condition of secular salvation. While *Deschooling Society* attracted a great deal of attention when it was first published, leading many of some of the most recognizable names in education (e.g., Paulo Freire, John Holt, Paul Goodman, and Joel Spring) to travel to Cuernavaca, Mexico to participate in seminars with Illich, his violation of this messianic rule of discursive inclusion led him to be subsequently excluded from educational discourse. That, in a nutshell, encapsulates the thesis of *Silencing Ivan Illich*. So, why revisit it?

In the first place, that was so many years ago. I completed it in its first iteration as my doctoral dissertation at the University of Cincinnati in 1991 under the direction of Joel Spring. Two years later, I published it in a slightly revised form with Austin and Winfield, but it went out of print when the publisher went out of business. None of that, of course, answers the question of what makes it worth revisiting almost 30 years later. As I saw it at the time, my work could have taken one of two different directions upon its completion. I could have moved in a positive direction of building upon Illich's ideas concerning what a deschooled society might look like and what would need to be done in order to achieve it. Alternatively, I could have chosen a negative path of using Illich's ideas to develop my own critique of compulsory schooling. I chose the latter.

In reflecting on this choice, I had my own personal axe to grind with our nation's educational system long before I could even articulate it. Though people look at me in disbelief when I tell them this, I volunteered to do a four-year enlistment in the U.S. Army shortly after earning my B.A. in English from Centre College of Kentucky. Various experiences during my military service led me to recognize just how badly my teachers (K-12 and college) had lied to me about American history and the role of the military in that history. I could have died because of those lies. I could have killed others because of those lies. My initial plan was to return to college in order to become a teacher and teach the truth. However, I spent my first class period in graduate school as a student in Joel Spring's course in the history of education. It only took that one class period with Joel to convince me that it wasn't just my teachers who lied. The entire system of compulsory schooling was created to spread lies on behalf of state and corporate power. That was the moment when I decided to go into higher education, which meant teacher education. However naively, I believed that I could make a larger difference in the world by helping teachers recognize what they were being asked to do in service to the corporate state so they could make other choices from themselves and their students.

So, that was the choice I made–the negative path of critical injury and judgement. I've spent more than a quarter century largely exposing the lies and propaganda of the school reforms undertaken since the 1980s that brought us the high stakes testing and school/teacher accountability measures that have since become permanent features of today's schools. Armed as I was with an Illichean critique of compulsory schooling when I entered the field, I never dreamed that I would end up defending that system. On top of criticizing the accountability measures meant to effect greater control over the work of teachers, however, I've also opposed the even more draconian push toward the privatization of schools. While teachers have limited amounts of control over their work as curriculum developers in the existing system public schools, particularly since high stakes testing arrived, privatization would alienate them from their labor even more dramatically by introducing the capitalist relation into the classroom. You sign a contract with a private corporation to teach what they want and how they want it taught. If not, you're out, and they find someone less interested in professional autonomy to replace you.

Moreover, in spite of my efforts to reveal the lies and propaganda of the modern school reform movement, and despite the efforts of many other very smart and talented people to fight those same reforms, the conditions of compulsory schooling have gotten worse since 1991. While I do not regret choosing the negative path of critical inquiry, I feel compelled at this juncture in my career to revisit that choice, and hence to revisit *Silencing Ivan Illich*.

What really compels me to want to take this step backward is a desire to move forward in a new direction, to choose that other path of positivity. I've felt this desire since just before leaving East Carolina University to come to Boise State six years ago. It started when I noticed while teaching courses on "diversity in education," how radically the standard multicultural emphasis on human differences puts our human commonalities out of focus. As I thought about all we share in common, I recognized a need to learn how to think at different scales, different scales of both time and space. Learning to think in this way takes us all, individually and collectively, down a notch. It's humbling to think of the cosmos, and how tiny and insignificant our "pale blue dot" of a planet actually is in the grander scheme of things. And this is not to sentimentalize anything, because learning to think on a cosmic scale should scare the hell out of us, perhaps literally. Think of how violent the forces were that created our sun and our planet. Think of how precarious our situation is on this planet. Thinking on a planetary scale, this thing we call earth only supports life, only allows for our existence because it happens to be situated just the right distance from the sun, and happens to be composed of just the right chemical elements that made the first single-celled organisms possible some 3.5 billion years ago. And yet the universe would not care one iota if we drove ourselves and every other species into total extinction. In the context of the diversity course, this big picture view of ourselves made me wonder what the fuck is wrong with us? I mean, think of how we treat each other! Think of how we've used these various ideologies (more lies) of sexism, classism, and racism to justify so much violence, death, and destruction, so much exploitation, and so much inequality and injustice. When I look at the world we've created, I have to ask myself: is this the kind of world we want to bequeath to our children? Shouldn't we be begging their forgiveness? Can't we do better than this? I have to believe that we can, and this belief not only supports whatever hope I have for the collective future of our species, but also propels me back to *Silencing Ivan Illich* in order to move beyond the negative and toward the positive.

Moving toward the positive in this instance means moving beyond questions of schooling. The questions I intend to ask in the follow-up book to this volume are far broader. They pertain to our capacities for what David Christian (2011) identifies as "collective learning." What we do with those capacities have and will dictate the future of our species. This is the conversation we need to have, and this is the conversation to which I hope to contribute in the next book that I hope to publish with Myers Education Press and throughout the next quarter century of my life.

Preface (1993 Edition)

Unlike flora and fauna, discourses do not enjoy the protection of any endangered species act. Discourses are fair game for the forces of repression, which often take very subtle forms. Subtle or not, these forces threaten the sort of diversity that provides a sort of ecological balance to a healthy discursive community by forcing transgressive discourses into a state of near-extinction. While the nature of these forces varies from one discursive community to another, this book examines the form that they have taken within the community of educational discourse. More specifically, informed by the archaeological method of textual analysis developed by Michel Foucault, I strive toward an understanding of the forces that excluded the discursive practices of Ivan Illich from that community. Governed by "the messianic principle of discursive inclusion," the discursive community of education mandates that "in order for a discourse to be accepted and seriously within this community, its rules of formation must constitute the school as a benevolent institution that can deliver the individual and/or society into a state of secular salvation." This principle has helped to create a pastoral image of school as an inherently beneficent institution. Regardless of the legitimacy of this image, the primary focus of this work is to demonstrate how the messianic principle guided the formation of various commentaries on Illich's writings that have reduced him to silence. Without valorizing Illich, the book attempts to remove the oppressive silence that has been imposed on his "voice," and, thereby, contribute toward a collective reconsideration of his message within the educational community. I argue here for a commitment from educator-scholars to dedicate themselves to greater discursive diversity within their field, a commitment that may carry over to the practices undertaken in the name of education.

Only time will tell if this book has its desired effect. Nonetheless, I owe a debt of gratitude to professor Spring for guiding me in its production.

Chapter One

To Explain an Exclusion

I HAD TWO purposes in mind when developing this work. On the one hand, I sought to contribute toward an understanding of a particular discourse that was originally enunciated in the late 1960s and early 1970s. On the other hand, and more importantly, I wanted to present a thorough understanding of how and why the discourse in question has since been reduced to silence. My investigation proceeds by asking two very general sorts of questions. First, what characteristics of the silenced discourse could have stimulated such a suffocating response? And second, what is the nature of the forces that have imposed such a penalty?

At a very fundamental level, these are questions of power and knowledge. Appropriating a Foucauldian mode of interpretive analysis, I view power and knowledge as being inseparable, and the significance of the relationship between the two is brought to the fore when discourse is conceptualized as a practice. The individual statement, then, is treated as the product of some discursive practice, an activity that delimits a field of objects, defines the legitimate perspective of the agent of knowledge, and fixes the norms for the elaboration of concepts and strategies. Moreover, the statement is the product of some specific discursive practice governed by particular rules of formation. These rules determine which objects, concepts, functions, and strategies are formed within discourse. They also determine how these discursive elements are formed. Such formations are never neutral, but are laden with power/knowledge relations.

To investigate the first of the aforementioned questions (what characteristics of the discourse in question could have stimulated such a suffocating response?), I take the rules of formation governing the discursive practice responsible for the statements in which the silenced discourse is embodied as the fundamental objects of my concern. Through an analysis of these rules and discursive elements that they give rise to, I reveal the characteristics rendering the discourse in question susceptible to being silenced and excluded from the discursive community of education.

Future references to the discourse in question, I shall use the terms primary discourse and core discourse, interchangeably. This facilitates a deeper understanding of its relationships to a whole series of other discourses that have proceeded from and have silenced it. It is useful to think of these as secondary discourses or peripheral discourses, for they constitute a sort of multi-layered discursive shell around the core. In general, however, I shall refer to them as commentaries.

What does it mean to comment on a discourse? First, it is to make that discourse speak again, to make that which has already been said speak again. Second, to comment on a discourse is to make it say something that it did not say before. Insofar as it speaks the never-before-said of an already-said, a commentary poses as a definitive restatement of some primary discourse. And, as a definitive restatement, it brings the already-said primary discourse into a condition of finality. It contains a covert declaration to the effect of, "Now that I have interpreted this discourse definitively, it has nothing more to say." It is in precisely this manner that the commentaries proceeding from the primary discourse have functioned to reduce it to silence.

As discourses, commentaries are also the textualized embodiments of discursive practices and are likewise guided by rules of formation. Though there may be some commonalities that can be established between the rules regulating the discursive practices behind the various commentaries, they each formulate the discourse *qua* object in their own unique fashion. In stating this, then, I am committed to analyzing a number of disparate discursive practices. This breadth of analysis is essential for adequately describing the full spectrum of silence-inducing forces that have been brought to bear on the primary discourse, though brevity does not allow for a complete genealogy of those practices.

The rules governing the formation of these commentaries legitimate different views of the primary discourse. These commentaries are characterized by different functions and adopt different strategies in bringing the primary discourse into a condition of finality, in restraining it, in impeding its circulation, and in restricting the wider consideration of its meanings. At the level of commentary, then, I am concerned with the control of discourse.

Michel Foucault (1982) has stated that:

> in every society the production of discourse is at once controlled, selected, organized, and redistributed according to a certain number of procedures, whose role is to avert its powers and its dangers, to cope with chance events, to evade its ponderous, awesome materiality. (p. 216)

And he identifies commentary as one means by which discourse is controlled (p. 221).

Insofar as I have yet to disclose the name of the writing subject, the appellation attached to the primary discourse, it becomes significant to describe a second mechanism of discursive control distinguished by Foucault. Although this mechanism operates neither universally across all fields of discourse nor constantly within these fields, at the present time within the discursive field of education, the author-function does, in fact, operate. This is one reason why the author-function is relevant to this discussion. Another reason of more immediate significance lies in the recognition that the author-function has enabled various commentators to contribute toward the exclusion of the primary discourse from the educational community.

That discourses have names attached to them at all should be recognized as a matter of historical contingency. According to Foucault (1977), "speeches and books were assigned real authors only when the author became subject to punishment and to the extent that her/his discourse was considered transgressive" (p. 124). While it is important to recognize that the most severe form of punishment (death) is still imposed upon those speakers and those authors whose transgressive discourses cannot be silenced by either marginalization or intimidation, the mechanisms of penality functioning within the discursive community of education and other academic disciplines do not generally operate directly upon the body of the writing subject. Rather, the forces of these mechanisms operate more typically upon the collective body of potential readers, those who may come into contact with a transgressive discourse.

Within the context of the primary discourse that is the object of this work, the author-function operates as a sign of transgression. In identifying this discourse as a practice that violates the rules governing their discursive practices within education and the community of educational discourse, the commentators whose works are described here have contributed toward its punishment by investing the name of the author with a pernicious aura. Because the dangerous individual's name is attached to the textualized embodiment of that discourse, having been invested with meanings assigned by others, the author functions on the surface of the text as an assemblage of "scarlet letters." It is a sign of the sinful. Those who have been made familiar with the name of the author as a dangerous individual will have, thereby, been forewarned of the perils that lurk within the text that rests behind the sign. The discourse itself has already been identified as a transgression by the potential reader without her/him ever having engaged it. Its meanings have, therefore, been effectively restricted, for their reputation, as invested in the name of the author, precedes them.

Various commentators have exerted similar forces of constraint and silence on Foucault's discourse/s by affiliating his name with transgression. In response to these forces, Foucault expresses a desire to have remained anonymous. He claims that this desire arose "out of nostalgia for a time when, being completely unknown, what I said had some chance of being heard. The surface contact with some possible reader was without a wrinkle. The effects of the books rebounded in unforeseen places and outlined forms I hadn't thought about" (1989, p. 193).

It also arose out of his recognition of how commentary and the author function work together to order, classify, distribute, and control discourse so as to avert its powers and its dangers. By enshrouding his discourse in anonymity, Foucault would have, in effect, been making an attempt to avert the powers and dangers that the author-function provides commentary *qua* discourse.

Though these powers and dangers have already been brought to bear on the discourse with which this project is concerned, though they have already reduced it to silence (it was out of print at the time that I wrote this in 1991), in the delineation of that discourse to be provided here I will attempt to lift the veil of oppressive silence from it in order to allow that discourse to speak again. To the extent that this involves an act of interpretation, I do not feign to be capable of reestablishing the unwrinkled surface and the primarily discourse in its originality. Short of this, I can only hope to make it "speak" again via a different method.

One component of this method involves isolating the statements by the primary discursive practice from the name of the author. This tactic will serve to avert the powers and dangers that previous commentators have exerted on it through their deployment of the author-function. While it is possible to avert the powers of previous commentators, the problem remains that, in making the primary discourse speak again, this work itself is a commentary. As stated in the opening paragraph, one of the purposes of this project is to determine the characteristics of the primary discourse that have stimulated the formation of a series of secondary discourses (commentaries) which have induced this silence. It is the characteristics which previous commentators have found to be transgressive of the rules governing "proper" educational discourse that I will focus on. The understanding I will contribute toward, therefore, is not devoid of its own set of rules of discursive formation. The extent to which the primary discourse can be liberated, then, is somewhat limited by the fact that all discursive practices involve the deployment of power/knowledge relations.

While acknowledging this problem, I do not intend to contribute toward the already dense shell of commentary that has suffocated the primary discourse. Neither do I intend, in my desire to re-enunciate that discourse, to valorize the writing subject who produced it. To do so would amount to little more than an inversion of the author-function. To invert the author-function by valorizing the writing subject would entail silencing those writing subjects who produced the secondary discourses surrounding it. It would mean situating the commentary that I am producing in competition with theirs.

I completely agree with Foucault when he states that "education may well be, as of right, the instrument whereby every individual, in a society like our own, can gain access to any kind of discourse" (1982, p. 227). The intent here, then, is not to challenge the validity of the arguments made by previous commentators, but rather to diminish the effects they have induced. In other words, I am not proposing that we should recast the hierarchy of discourse that exists within the field of education by situating a previously excluded discourse at the top of that hierarchy. I am simply arguing that we should refrain from conceptualizing that field of discourse in hierarchical terms. In order that education can become the sort of instrument envisioned by Foucault, all discourses must be granted inclusion within its discursive field. As it stands now, however, education is but yet another means for controlling discourse:

> In its distribution, in what it permits and in what it prevents. [education] follows the well trodden battle-lines of social conflict. Every educational system is a political means of maintaining or of modifying the appropriation of discourse, with the knowledge and the powers it carries with it. (Foucault, 1982, p. 227)

When conceptualized in hierarchical terms, the discursive field of education can be viewed as being constructed from "politically correct" discourses at the top of the hierarchy and "politically incorrect" discourses at the bottom. By no means am I suggesting that there is any broad consensus within any given field of academe, especially within education. Different individuals within the academy have different definitions of which discourses qualify as politically correct or incorrect. Nevertheless, whether it is affected by the faculty of an academic program as a whole, or whether it is affected by a single mentor, the socialization of the student into some version of "politically correct" discourse or set of discourses entails learning to associate names with those discourses. More often than not, the result of this socialization is that apprentices learn whose discourses they should appropriate in order to receive legitimation themselves. Their legitimation is cast not in terms of their competence as productive writing and speaking subjects, but in terms of their political correctness. Moreover, apprentices are socialized to choose the foundations of their own discursive practices carefully.

Being socialized into a discursive community also involves being socialized to recognize certain other discourses as "politically incorrect." Names, of course, associated with the discourses as well. And, it is often the case that names themselves come to represent transgressions. An apprentice can, thereby, easily claim to reject the theory put forth by some writing subject without ever having examined the discourse which elaborates that theory. The direct association of a name with transgression impedes the proliferation of discourse and restricts the full consideration of its meanings. In other words, apprentices are socialized away from certain discursive practices as they are socialized into others. Even when they are encouraged to investigate transgressive texts, they are forewarned of the improprieties that await them. If a pernicious discourse is to be cited in the work of the apprentice, that citation must be made for the sheer purpose of allowing the legitimate discourse to demonstrate its efficacy as a vehicle for commentary. Hence, both commentary and the author function are of extreme importance at the level of discursive appropriation. Due to this significance, I have chosen to leave anonymous the writing subject who produced the primary discourse that has been labelled within current educational discourse as "politically incorrect."

Therefore, the significance that I attach to this project lies not within the primary discourse itself, but in its exclusion from the broader field of educational discourse. I want to describe the discursive forces originating from within that field that have resulted in this exclusion. At the heart of this work, therefore, is deeper level of concern for the more universal rules of formation with the discursive community of education that permit some discourses to be included within its boundaries while excluding other discourses. It becomes useful, then, to think of the discursive field of education not as a hierarchy, but rather as an archive in which some discourses are included and others are excluded. This makes it possible to describe the method that I will employ in investigating the commentaries activated by those discursive practices comprising the archive and the primary discourse that they have excluded from that archive as an archaeology. Though such a description is in some sense problematic, I will attempt to recast this description through an elaboration of the methodology that I have adopted in the next chapter.

References

Foucault, M. (1977). What is an author? In D.F. Bouchard (ed.), *Language, counter-memory and practice: Selected essays and interviews with Michel Foucault* (113–138). Ithaca, NY: Cornell University Press.

Foucault, M. (1982). *The archaeology of knowledge and the discourse on language*. New York, NY: Pantheon Books.

Foucault, M. (1989). The masked philosopher. In S. Lotringer (ed.), *Foucault live: Interviews 1961–84* (302–307). New York, NY: Semiotext(e).

CHAPTER TWO

Theoretico-Activism

I HAVE PURPOSEFULLY chosen, as one of the central objects of this analysis, a primary discourse that has been excluded from the archive of educational discourse. My motivation for having selected such a discourse is that it provides me with the opportunity to investigate the rules of discursive formation from which the commentaries that have facilitated this exclusion emerge. From this investigation, I expect to be able to define a dominant principle of inclusion that regulates the composition of that archive, and a concomitant principle of exclusion that prohibits certain discourses from attaining any degree of legitimacy within educational debate.

In the closing paragraph of the previous chapter, I stated that there are certain difficulties involved in drawing an analogy between the methodology that I employ in conducting this investigation and archaeology. Like the methodology itself, the term archaeology is borrowed from Michel Foucault's *The Archaeology of Knowledge* (1982), which was his account of his own mode of analysis. Foucault used the term archaeology to signify a

> description of the archive…, the set of discourses actually pronounced; and this set of discourses is envisaged not only as a set events which would have taken place once and for all and which would remain in abeyance, in the limbo or purgatory of history, but to provide the possibility of appearing in other discourses. (1989, p. 45)

Though it enabled him to distinguish his mode of analysis from that employed by historians of ideas, Foucault's discomfort with the implications of describing his endeavors as archaeological (as if he were involved in a process of excavating facts) caused him to later drop the term from his language of methodological self-representation. He found that, along with its essentialist implications, it did not adequately communicate what he was trying to accomplish through his investigations. To ascribe greater specificity and accuracy to his description of his own discursive practice, he came to characterize his methodology as *theoretico-active*.

What, then, was Foucault attempting to accomplish by developing this method of analysis? More importantly, what am I attempting to accomplish by adopting it? To address the latter and more immediately significant question, I must elaborate the *a priori* assumptions inherent within theoretico-activism.

First, it is important to recall that I described the two principal questions guiding my investigation as being questions of power and knowledge. I also stated that it is possible to recognize that power and knowledge are inseparable when the 'statement,' as a conceptual category, is understood to be the product of a specific discursive practice guided by its own unique configuration of rules of formation. This conceptualization works in conjunction, as intimated in the preceding sentence, with a conceptualization of "discourse" as a practice. Furthermore, the rules of formation regulating a given discursive practice determine which objects, concepts, functions, and strategies are formed within the statements which that practice gives rise to. These rules also determine how these discursive elements are formed. Every act of discourse involves the activation of some set of rules that govern the formation of the knowledge contained within the statement/s to be produced by that discourse. Therefore, power, as manifested in the rules of formation, becomes inseparable from the knowledge generated by the practice that is regulated by those rules.

Second, and concurrently, just as power and knowledge are conceptualized as being inseparable, the traditional distinction between theory and practice is blurred within theoretico-activism. Rather than viewing theory as being anterior to practice, a theoretico-active approach to discourse treats theory and practice at the same level. Not only is theory conceptualized as being within practice, it is conceptualized as a practice in its own right. Even to theorize silently to oneself is to engage in a discursive practice and involves the deployment of rules of formation and, therefore, power. One must "think" within the categories provided by the rules of formation that are inherent in the language that one "thinks" with.

Third, the starting point of theoretico-active analysis is the isolated and individualized statement. Keep in mind the *a priori* assumption that the statement is the product of a specific discursive practice guided by its own unique configuration of rules of formation, and that these rules determine how and which objects, concepts, functions, and strategies are formed within the statement. It is this assumption which prompts the central task to be undertaken in theoretico-active analysis, which is to suspend the unity of the individualized statement.

This suspension entails a refusal to view language as being the conduit between the world and the human mind. Instead, the theoretico-active approach involves perceiving the act of naming something in the world as the most rudimentary exercise of power. Therefore, suspending the unity of the statement amounts to a refusal to take for granted the objects, concepts, functions, and strategies that are contained within a given statement. To suspend the unity of the statement is to perceive, at least initially, the field of discursive elements as a system of dispersion. When entering a system of dispersion, from a Foucauldian perspective, one should begin searching for the rules that regulate the formation of these elements.

In recognition that these discursive elements are formed by the practice of discourse, the second task of a theoretico-active analysis is to explain the rules governing their formation. Again, it is significant to be reminded that the starting point of theoretico-active analysis is the isolated and individualized statement. It is isolated in the sense that it is isolated from its originating subject. The theoretico-activist is not concerned with the psychological condition or the mental state of the writing subject who produced the statement. The statement is also individualized in the sense that it is separated from other statements contained within a text. Once the rules governing the formation of a statement's discursive elements are established, the unity within the individualized statement can be reestablished and the theoretico-activist can begin attempting to detect possible unities between the statements within a text and the possible unities between the texts within an *oeuvre*.

Prior to the establishment of the regularities between and within statements, however, it is necessary to suspend the unity of the individual texts that represent the embodiment of the discourse. Foucault (1982) states that

> the book is not simply the object that one holds in one's hands; and it cannot remain in the little parallelepiped that contains it: its unity is variable and relative...it is caught up in a system of references to other books, other texts, other sentences: it is a node within a network. (p. 23)

And prior to the suspension of the unity of the book/text, the unity of the *oeuvre* must be suspended. Why should this unity be suspended? "What could be more simple?" Foucault (1982) asks. "A collection of texts that can be designated by the sign of a proper name" (p. 23). In spite of its apparent simplicity as a unity, Foucault contends that to assume the nonproblematic unity of an author's *oeuvre*, the unified collectivity of an author's works, is to admit

> that there is a level...at which the *oeuvre* emerges, in all its fragments, even its smallest, most inessential ones, as the expression of the thought, the expertise, the imagination, or the unconsciousness of the author, or, indeed, of the historical determinations that acted upon her/him. (Foucault, 1982, p. 24).

The establishment of any unity, however, is the result of an interpretive operation. The *oeuvre*, therefore, "can be regarded neither as an immediate unity, nor as a certain unity, nor as a homogeneous unity" (Foucault, 1982, p. 24). In suspending the *oeuvre*, the unity that is ordinarily provided to the set of texts by the sign of a proper name is interrupted. Any unity that might exist between the texts that are the manifestations of the primary discourse must be developed through the interpretive processes of the theoretico-active analysis initiated in the third chapter.

There is one further characteristic of theoretico-activism's conceptualization of the statement that holds relevance for this project. This relevance has to do with the anonymity in which I have shrouded the writing subject who produced the primary discourse. Not only does the theoretico-active conceptualization of the statement recognize no set of referential objects that are grounded in "reality," it also recognizes no originating subject. The referential subject of the statement is constituted by the very rules that regulate the formation of the elements within the statement. Instead of being cast as a point of a statement's origin, the subject of a statement is defined by the same laws that make the statement possible. The position of the statement's subject can, therefore, be filled by any number of different individuals. It is this quality which makes statements repeatable and which enable me to make those statements in question speak again. Thus, the question of "who is speaking?" becomes irrelevant from a theoretico-active perspective.

As stated in the first chapter, it is through an investigation of the primary discourse and commentaries that have excluded it from the archive of educational discourse that I hope to determine the dominant principles of inclusion and exclusion regulating that archive. The question that needs to be addressed in the remainder of this chapter, then, is "How can theoretico-activism contribute toward this determination?"

I will be dealing with two sets of texts as the objects of this theoretico-active analysis. Firstly, there are the texts in which the primary discourse is embodied. Because these texts are the products of the discursive practice of a single writing subject, they can be cumulatively referred to as an *oeuvre*. Not all of the texts that the writing subject has produced will be discussed here, however. What criteria guided me in deciding which texts to include in this partial *oeuvre*? First, I am interested in those texts produced by discursive practices which transgress the principle of inclusion regulating the archive of educational discourse. Therefore, those texts in which the primary discursive practice forms the school as one of its objects will be included within this partial *oeuvre*. However, because there is an exceptionally high degree of significance to be drawn from those texts in which the writing subject forms the church as the object of discourse, these texts are also included in the partial *oeuvre*.

It should be obvious that, given the description of the theoretico-active method already provided in this chapter, the unity of this partial *oeuvre*, as well as the unity of the texts within it, must be suspended. Once this deep level of theoretico-active analysis is reached, I can begin describing the rules of formation that govern the manner in which the discursive practice at work in the primary discourse goes about constructing its objects, concepts, functions, and strategies. From the point at which these rules of formation are established, the unity within and between these statements may be reestablished. Therefore, the unity of the texts and also the *oeuvre* may be reestablished, as well. What is of the most fundamental importance, however, is the nature of the rules of formation, for it is these rules which violate the principle of inclusion that regulates the archive of educational discourse.

This brings us to a second set of texts to be subjected to theoretico-active analysis. These texts are the commentaries that exercise the power of exclusion from within this archive. They are formed by discursive practices whose rules of formation conform to that archive's principle of inclusion and function to enforce its principle of exclusion. Because they are not produced by the same writing subject, these texts/commentaries do not constitute an *oeuvre*. Therefore, there is no *oeuvre* whose unity needs to be suspended as the theoretico-active analysis moves toward establishing the rules of formation governing the construction of the discursive elements within the individualized statements produced by the secondary discursive practices.

Again, it is the nature of these rules of formation which holds the greatest significance for this current work. And it is through theoretico-active analysis that one can establish these rules. This is because each of the commentaries contains a rule of formation in keeping with the dominant principle of inclusion that facilitates the incorporation of their respective discursive practices within the archive of educational discourse. And it is this rule of formation which embodies the archive's dominant principle of inclusion violated by the primary discourse.

In other words, there is an object that is formed by both the primary discursive practice and the secondary discursive practices. However, the rules governing these discourses formulate the object in a different fashion. Therefore, it is formed, in some sense, as a completely different object across these discourses. But the manner in which this object is formed by the rules governing the primary discursive practice is in violation of a fundamental assumption contained within the archive of educational discourse's principle of inclusion and, therefore, the rules of formation that guide the discursive practices manifested in the individual commentaries. Moreover, the rules of formation generating this object within the primary discourse are incommensurable with both the rules of formation which govern its construction in the commentaries and the archive's principle of inclusion. Therefore, because of these concurrent violations, that primary discourse has been excluded from the archive and, thereby, silenced within the discursive community of education. The object to which I have been referring is the school.

I began this chapter by claiming to have purposefully chosen a primary discourse that has been excluded from the archive of educational discourse. I have since explicated how the theoretico-active method of analysis enables me to reveal that this exclusion is the result of the school being formed within the primary discourse in a manner that violates the archive's dominant principle of inclusion. Chapter Three describes this formation and its relationship to a series of other discursive elements that are formed within the statements proper to the primary discourse. Chapter Four delineates how the principle of inclusion that dominates the archive of educational discourse informs the various commentaries which have functioned as exclusionary practices, how they have silenced that primary discourse because of the transgression it commits in forming the school as it does. In this manner, I will be able to determine the dominant principle of inclusion that regulates the composition of the archive of educational discourse, and a concomitant principle of exclusion that prohibits certain discourses from attaining any degree of legitimacy within educational debate.

Before moving forward with the discussion of the primary discourse in Chapter Three, I would like to address an argument that might be raised to question the significance of the theoretico-active approach to textual analysis. According to this argument, what would result from a theoretico-active analysis of the primary discourse and the commentaries that have acted to silence it is a very protracted and convoluted literature review. Further, such a review could only produce a revelation of the various subjectivities that have excluded another subjectivity from educational discourse. But this is precisely what is being avoided in my adoption of Foucault's theoretico-activism.

This mode of analysis gives us a new language with which to describe the construction of knowledge. To speak of the socially, politically, and culturally influenced practice of knowledge construction in terms of subjectivity is to acknowledge the existence of its opposite (objectivity). Therefore, the language of subjectivity, which speaks of biases, prejudices, and opinions, cannot help but refer to the language of objectivity, which speaks of neutral observational methods, neutral knowledge, facts, and timeless truth. The language of theoretico-activism avoids this trap by speaking only of the power/knowledge relations that are inherent in the formation of discourse. It acknowledges that all discursive practices including its own, are rule-governed.

A further question emerges here that concerns the potential advantages to be gained from disrupting the certainty that human beings have become so comfortable with in qualifying their knowledge while, concurrently, disestablishing the dualism of subjectivity versus objectivity. The response to this question is twofold. On the one hand, in doing away with the traditional dualism of subjectivity versus objectivity, we can turn our backs to those who would argue that social and political decisions should be based on "facts by those who have the 'facts' straight." The solidity of a reality against which to bounce those "facts" has begun to crumble. Though the situation that this leaves us in is troublesome, it offers us the opportunity to achieve a greater degree of egalitarianism in our negotiation of social and political issues. Without a solid reality as a point of reference for the validation of our knowledge claims, we can more forcefully frame our political arguments within the framework of values.

On the other hand, the disestablishment of the subjectivity versus objectivity dualism opens up a broader discursive space. Again, without a solid reality as point of reference for the validation of our knowledge claims, a wider variety of discourses are afforded the freedom to circulate and to have their meanings taken under consideration by a wider variety of people. No discourse can be excluded from discursive space on the basis of its lack of neutrality. But this is, of course, contingent on the formation of a new value, the value of discursive freedom which places a premium on education as defined by Foucault (1982): "the instrument by which any individual, in a society like our own, can gain access to any kind of discourse" (p. 227). It is this value, insofar as this work represents an attempt to re-enunciate a discourse that has been excluded from the archive of educational discourse that I am most concerned with upholding and promoting.

References

Foucault, M. (1982). *The archaeology of knowledge and the discourse on language.* New York, NY: Pantheon Books.

Foucault, M. (1989). The archaeology of knowledge. In S. Lotringer (ed.), *Foucault live: Interviews 1961–84* (57–64). New York, NY: Semiotext(e).

CHAPTER THREE

To Deny the Pastoral

The Primary Discourses

The central task of this chapter is to determine the rules of discursive practice that form the school as an object of this primary discourse. To accomplish this task, I have selected just two texts to include in the partial *oeuvre*. As described in the previous chapter, I must suspend the unity of this partial *oeuvre* as well as that of the texts within it in order to reach the deep level of the individualized statement. It is at this level that I will conduct the theoretico-active analysis of the rules of formation that govern the discursive practice manifested in the texts to be considered here. To report on the suspension of the unity of every individualized statement within these texts, of course, would make for toilsome reading. I shall therefore limit the scope of these sections to a description of the rules of formation that are most pertinent to the above-mentioned task.

The first rules of formation to be discussed here, however, do not form the school as one of their objects. As intimated earlier, many of the texts that have been produced by the writing subject are constructed by statements that form the church as the central object. One such text has been included in this partial *oeuvre* for analysis. An explication of the full significance of the discursive relationship between the church and the school will be reserved for later in the chapter. It remains necessary, however, in order to justify the ensuing discussion of the church, to mention that the significance of this relationship is directly related to the principle of inclusion violated by the primary discourse which has resulted in its exclusion from the archive of educational discourse.

Before moving on to the description of the pertinent rules of formation, it is also meaningful to note that, though the texts to be subjected to theoretico-active analysis are linked to the gesture of writing, they are also linked, as are all texts, to the articulation of speech. The gestures responsible for the textualized discursive practices embodied in the statements of these texts, then, cannot be disassociated from the unrecorded discursive events from which they emerge. This is especially true of the statements whose rules of formation develop the church as their object. The first text to fall under analysis is registered within a field of discourse as a reaction to certain events and practices, both discursive and non-discursive, tied to a dilemma confronted by the Catholic Church's Archdiocese in New York City during the 1950s.

Text One

There are many churches formed within this text, and this variety of churches is formed in accordance with two different sets of rules. One set of rules is responsible for the formation of the church as a Concept. These rules also impact upon a further set of rules governing the formation of the church as an Object of the primary discourse that is manifested in the text. In accordance with one of the rules from the first set, the church is conceptualized as an institution which is the *object* of cultural forces. The cultural forces that are exerted against the church, or any other institution, largely determine the manner in which the church conceptualizes its relationships to individuals. The other rule that operates within this text to form the church as a concept constructs the church as the *subject* of cultural forces. The institutional church *qua object* is influenced by cultural forces which shape its perception of its relationship to individuals. In turn, these same cultural forces that invest themselves in the institutional church are transformed as they pass through the church. The church, in the specificity of its social function, acts as a filter of cultural forces on its way to becoming a subject which exerts cultural forces of its own. The forces exerted by the institutional church invest themselves in individuals to influence the manner in which they conceptualize their relationship to the church. Therefore, it can be stated that the institutional church itself does not hold power, but rather that the power manifested in cultural forces flows through the church.

A deeper understanding of the rules which govern the double-formation of the church as a concept within *Text One* can be gleaned from an account of the leverage that they exercise upon the rules that govern the formation of the church as an object in this same text. There are two churches that are formed as objects within this text: the institutional church in North America, and the institutional church in Puerto Rico. Within the context of its conceptual status as an object of cultural forces, the North American church is formed as having been heavily influenced by European culture. After all, the North American church, although shaped by forces that are distinctly North American, was transplanted from European soil. Due to the influence of European culture in shaping the North American church as a social formation, the writing subject explains that European immigrants had little difficulty in being assimilated into its institutional practices. Their perceived relationship with the institutional church in Europe had been cast by a similar set of cultural forces as those exerted by the institutional church in North America. As a result, the European immigrants are said to have had little problem fulfilling the North American church's expectations of them as Catholics.

However, within the context of its conceptual status as an object of cultural forces, the institutional church in Puerto Rico was shaped by a set of cultural forces that were distinct from those at work in both Europe and North America. In the first place, as a largely agrarian society, Puerto Rico's population was widely dispersed throughout the island's interior. Secondly, churches there were few and far between, priests visited local chapels only on rare occasions, and there were very few Puerto Ricans in the priesthood. It is under these circumstances, as the subject of cultural forces, that the institutional church in Puerto Rico is formed within *Text One* as having played only a minor role in the daily lives of Puerto Ricans. They had irregular and infrequent contact with the institutional church and, therefore, with the cultural forces exerted by it. While the Puerto Ricans considered themselves to be devoutly Catholic, they did not sense that they needed to attend Mass every Sunday, to have a priest baptize their children or preside over their marriages in order to demonstrate their spiritual commitment to the faith.

It is upon the basis of the formation of these two churches and their respective relationship to their parishioners that the writing subject moves to explain why the Puerto Rican immigrants did not fulfill the North American church's expectations of them as Catholics. It is because they did not meet these expectations, because they did not conceptualize their own relationship to the church in the same manner that the European immigrants had that the Puerto Rican immigrants presented the Catholic Church's Archdiocese in New York with a dilemma.

The question that needs to be addressed, then, concerns the nature of the proper relationship between the individual and the institutional church as conceptualized by North American and European parishioners. The writing subject's formation of the Puerto Rican parishioner's conceptualization of this relationship has already been described. Because this writing subject does not directly address the European and/or North American parishioner's perception of this relationship, we are forced to describe this conceptualization through negative analysis. That is, we need to draw inferences from this text at the point where the North American church's view of the dilemma posed by the Puerto Rican immigrants emerges. One such point can be located within the following statement:

> Many U.S. Catholics are used to a wide variety of national customs in national parishes and a great difference in practices among various ethnic groups; when faced with the lack of 'practice' [emphasis added] of their faith by Puerto Ricans, they might be tempted to identify them with some other foreign group in whom the effects of a different background show up in similar behavior, or might deny altogether that Puerto Ricans are Catholic. (Illich, 1970b, p. 39)

The key phrase in this passage is "the lack of 'practice'." Practice is even situated within quotation marks for emphasis. Given the formation of the

Puerto Ricans' relationship to the institutional church in their homeland as a relationship characterized by little contact between the institutional church and the Puerto Rican people, the significance of the phrase "lack of 'practice'" becomes evident.

A lack of practice means a lack of contact with the institutional church. It suggests a failure to attend Mass on a regular and frequent basis, a failure to demand that a priest baptize one's children. Moreover, it intimates a failure to engage in the practice of Catholicism as defined by the North American Church.

It is intimated in the above passage, drawn from *Text One*, then, that in both North America and Europe, parishioners derive their sense of Catholicism from regular and frequent contact with the church as an institution. For North Americans and Europeans to be considered truly Catholic, in both their own eyes and the eyes of their fellow "Catholics," regular and frequent contact with the institutional church was compulsory. Therefore, it is possible to state that North Americans and Europeans conceptualized their proper relationship to the institutional church as a relationship characterized by a regular and frequent contact that is mandated by the church in order for them to be granted spiritual salvation after death.

At this point, it becomes possible to discern how the writing subject who produced *Text One* forms the dilemma that the North American church saw itself presented with by the Puerto Rican immigrants. Firstly, the cultural forces which shaped the North American church's conceptualization of its relationship to its individual parishioners and, therefore the intended effects of the forces that it exerts on them, were foreign to the Puerto Ricans. They did not recognize that contact with the institutional church was requisite to their sense of Catholicism or for their spiritual salvation. Secondly, in its status as a subject of cultural forces, the North American church conceptualized this situation as a dilemma because the cultural forces that it exerts on individuals carried no efficacy for the Puerto Ricans. This dilemma, as it was conceptualized by the institutional church in North America, could only be resolved through the formation of tactics by which the Puerto Rican immigrants could be brought into the fold of the North American style of Catholicism. That is, tactics were required that would fulfill the North American church's strategy of making them want to come into contact with the institutional church, to make them dependent on that institution for their spirit of Catholicism.

At this point, it is significant to point out that the rules of formation guiding *Text One* in its construction of its discursive elements are responsible for the creation of a particular function that operates at a point between the North American church and the Puerto Rican people. This function can best be characterized as a diplomatic function and is formed within *Text One* in conjunction with the formation of a particular strategy. The writing subject appears within this text as a diplomat who functions in accordance with a strategy of intervention on behalf of a people (the Puerto Rican immigrants) who are not dependent on the church for their religious belief and their spiritual salvation, and an intervention which challenges the church *qua* subject of cultural forces in its demand for such dependence. Moreover, this strategy of intervention represents an effort to deflect the cultural forces exerted by the institutional church in North America upon the Puerto Rican immigrants.

It now becomes crucial to consider the nature of those forces at work within North American culture. Insofar as the rules of discursive formation that operate in this text conceptualize the church as a subject of cultural forces, it is important to situate the formation of the North American church and the Puerto Rican church as objects of this discourse within the context of this conceptualization. It is here that it is possible to discern that European immigrants and North American parishioners desire contact with the institutional church because of the nature of the cultural forces exerted by the North American church, and that the Puerto Ricans do not desire contact with this institutional church because cultural forces exerted by the Puerto Rican church were, at least, *qua*ntitatively different from those exerted by the North American church. Therefore, there is some *qua*lity inherent in the forces exerted by the North American church which strives to produce a certain level of desire within individuals for contact with the institutional church. To fully explain this special *qua*lity, we need to briefly step outside of the primary discourse.

Foucault (1982) notes that "Christianity is the only religion which has organized itself as a Church," that is, as an institution. As an institution, the church "postulates in principle that certain individuals can, by their religious *qua*lity, serve others…as pastors" (p. 214). As the agents of this institution, these pastors exercise *pastoral power*, the ultimate aim of which is to "assure individual salvation in the next world. They must be prepared to sacrifice themselves for the life and salvation of the flock." The pastoral power of the institutional church, which flows through these individuals as its agents, is not directed just toward the community as a whole, but toward "each individual in particular, during [her/his] entire life—It implies a knowledge of the conscience and the ability to direct it" (p. 214).

Returning now to the primary discourse, this pastoral power is the dominant cultural force exerted by the North American church to render individuals dependent on its institutional forms. It directs their consciousness by convincing them that spiritual salvation can only be guaranteed to them if they establish regular and frequent contact with the institutional church. They come to know themselves as Catholics through this contact. Therefore, their conscience is clear only insofar as they are in regular and frequent contact with the institutional church in their efforts to achieve spiritual salvation. Their conscience, on the other hand, is directed to experience guilt if that contact is ever broken. The Puerto Rican immigrants frustrated this pastoral power of the North American church, because they had not come into contact with it in their native land.

The infrequent contact of the Puerto Rican immigrants with the institutional church in North America was seen by the church as a "lack of 'practice.'" Unlike European immigrants, the Puerto Ricans did not experience any desire to establish the sort of contact with the institutional church that the North American church would recognize as the proper practice of Catholicism which would lead them to their spiritual salvation. Because the United States Constitution guarantees a separation of church and state, the church could not force the Puerto Ricans into contact with its institutional forms any more than it could have forced those of European descent into such contact.

The major difference between the Puerto Rican immigrants and those from Europe lie in the Europeans' desire for contact with the institutional church and its practices. That the Puerto Ricans experienced no such desire attests to the fact that desire for contact with the institutional church in order to realize spiritual salvation is not an authentically human desire; it is not an inborn trait. It is, however, desire that is demanded by the institutional church in North America. And this demand is the result of the cultural forces that are exerted upon the institutional church within the context of its conceptual status as an object.

For the writing subject who functions in this text as a diplomat to intervene on behalf of the Puerto Rican immigrants, such demands are deplorable in that they render individuals dependent upon institutions. We will later see how similar cultural forces further create such demands on individuals by other institutions in North America, and how these demands render individuals dependent on those other institutions for reasons other than the promise of spiritual salvation. We will also be able to discern from *Text Two* how the writing subject conceptualizes this notion of dependence with regard to relationships between individuals, as well as the consequences of such dependent relationships. Before proceeding with this analysis, however, I will attempt to explain how the pastoral power which induces dependence among individuals in their relationships to institutions has become dispersed throughout modern society. This explanation will enable the reader to recognize more concretely the connection between the church and the school, and how this connection is related to the principle of inclusion that governs educational discourse. Once again, this requires moving outside of the primary discourse.

The Dispersion of Pastoral Power

Though the church is no longer the dominant institution that it once was, pastoral power continues to function and not only within the church. Foucault argues that the pastoral power once associated exclusively with the Church has become dispersed throughout the social body and now functions through a multitude of institutions that are often either a component of or affiliated with the modern state. Applying Foucault's argument to the primary discourse, then, in its dispersion beyond the confines of the institutional church, this form of power has undergone a major transformation. The pastoral power that flows from modern institutions has a strategy that differs from that which was exercised by the church to the end of the seventeenth century. Foucault claims that it no longer functions to promise the individual a form of salvation in the next world, the world after death. Rather, he contends that it functions to promise the individual and/or society some form of salvation in this world. "And in this context," he argues, "the word salvation takes a different meaning: health, well-being (that is, sufficient wealth, standard of living), security, protection against accidents" (Foucault, 1982, p. 215). In the social realm, the form of salvation projected to individuals is peculiar to the institution through which pastoral power flows. In the discursive realm of education, the form of salvation that is promised is determined by the rules of formation which govern the particular discursive practice issuing the promise.

As the agencies of pastoral power have grown more numerous, so too has the number of pastoral agents increased. In a text that will not be discussed at any great length here, the writing subject of the primary discourse with which we are concerned forms the institutional church as "the world's largest non-governmental bureaucracy" (Illich, 1970a, p. 71). It is significant to note, then, that William Brock (1990), the former Labor Secretary of the United States, points out that "in the city of New York there are more school administrators than there are in all of France, In the state of New York, there are more [school] administrators than there are in all of the European Community (EC), and the EC has twelve countries and 320 million people" (p. 14).

For an institution like the school to create a large number of pastoral agents contributes toward a greater dispersion of its pastoral power throughout the social body in an attempt to maximize the number of contacts that can be established between that institution and the individual bodies that it seeks to render dependent. This seeking to establish material contact with bodies and to "know" individual consciences provides, for Foucault, evidence of pastoral powers' individualizing capacity. It produces a desire within the individual to have more and more contact with the institution in order to increase her/his chances of realizing the condition of salvation that was promised.

The *disciplinary power* that ensues from the establishment of this contact is more totalizing in the sense that, by manipulating individuals to desire contact with the same institutions, it aims toward the cohesion of the social body. Disciplinary power strives toward "generating forces, making them grow, and ordering them" (Foucault,1980a, p. 136). Through techniques, controls, and normalizing procedures, the power relations which emerged with the liberal-democracies of the eighteenth and nineteenth centuries are production oriented, not repression oriented. They aim for the production of a certain type of individual and the homogenization of individuals who will voluntarily gravitate toward institutions, disciplining them into dependency. According to Foucault (1980b):

> these new techniques of power were needed to grapple with the phenomena of population, in short, to undertake the administration,

> control, and direction of the accumulation of men (the economic system that promotes the accumulation of capital and the system of that ordains the accumulation of men were, from the seventeenth century on, correlated, and inseparable phenomena). (p. 125)

In order to achieve maximum efficiency, the mechanism and the supporting ideology of disciplinary power have had to remain hidden. Therefore, by providing modern institutions with beneficent images, pastoral power can be said to function as a mode of concealment.

At a discursive level, the pastoral power that flows from the school *qua* modern institution manifests itself as a particular rule of discursive formation. Appropriating C.A. Bowers' (1967) well-articulated description of what he describes as the "messianic tradition in American education," one of the cardinal rules that serves to define the discursive community of education is formed by the idea that universal education/schooling must be held up as the most assured method to "bring into being a more ideal social order or raise the individual to a higher level of moral existence" (p. 203). Though various pedagogical methods and theoretical treatments of education have been put forth which differ greatly from one another and are not elevated above all criticisms, they are normally guaranteed inclusion within the discursive community of education only if they do not deviate from this messianic principle. Similarly, rival political factions within this community are free to reject a discourse that conforms to the messianic principle on more specific grounds established by their own particular rules of discursive formation. Nevertheless, while some may be more marginalized than others, all discursive practices that conform to this "messianic principle of discursive inclusion" are guaranteed admission to the archive of educational discourse.

In rejecting all pastoral images of the school, and in disclaiming the potential for the various forms of secular salvation that are promised by those who are dependent on the school at a conceptual level, the primary discourse violates this messianic principle of inclusion that has governed educational discourse since the rise of public schooling. This rejection and the significance of the connections between the church and the school are most evident in the formation of the statement within the text about to be subjected to theoretico-active analysis which proclaims that schooling has become the "world religion of a modernized proletariat which make futile promises of salvation to the poor of the technological age" (Illich, 1970b, p. 18).

Text Two

The theoretico-active analysis of *Text One* began by calling the reader's attention to the rules which conceptualize the church as a multiplicitous institution. Similar sets of rules are active here in *Text Two*. Just as there are many churches formed within *Text One*, there is a multiplicity of schools formed within this text. Also similar to *Text One*, the multiplicity of schools formed in *Text Two* are produced in accordance with two different sets of rules. One set of rules is responsible for the formation of the school as a concept. These rules also impact upon a further set of rules which govern the formation of the school as an object of the primary discourse that is manifested in the text.

The first set of discursive rules of formation conceptualize the school within the context of an institutional spectrum. At the negative end of this spectrum, the writing subject emerges within the text as a critical functionary to develop the concept of the manipulative institution. At the positive end of the spectrum, the writing subject takes on a revolutionary function in developing the concept of the *convivial institution*. Because this book is most concerned with the manner in which the discourse manifested here in *Text Two* transgresses the messianic principle of inclusion, the bulk of this theoretico-active analysis will be applied to the rule which develops the concept of the manipulative institution and how that rule impacts on the rules which form the school as an object.

At the most general level, the modern school, in accordance with the first above-mentioned rule, is conceptualized within *Text Two* as the paradigm of a manipulative institution. This conceptualization strongly influences the ensuing formations of the school as an object of this discourse. The rules governing these formations depict the modern school, simultaneously, as a type of medicine show, as a new brand of church, and as a sort of factory. These three formations often overlap and complement one another. They operate together in challenging the messianic principle of inclusion that segregates or excludes from the archive of educational discourse the discursive practice that forms them. As the embodiments of manipulative practices, the "three faces" of the schools each emerge from the point at which education, as a value, is displaced and misconceived.

There is, then, another set of rules here which govern the formation of the concept of education. Education is conceptualized as an authentically human value that emerges from the authentically human need to learn. However, under the influence of its conceptualization as a manipulative institution that shapes its formation as a factory, the school obfuscates the origins of this value and, therefore, distorts the manner in which it is property served. Moreover, the school *qua* factory manipulates individuals so as to prevent them from recognizing education as an authentically human value. Instead, it encourages them to adopt education as an institutionalized value, which is presented by the writing subject as a myth.

In general terms, the writing subject denies that either the product of an institutional process or the institutional process itself can constitute a value. The concept of "institution" is formed here as the site of a specific productive process. An institution may serve or purport to serve a properly human value; it may meet or purport to meet some human need. However, an institution cannot truly contain, produce, market, or distribute a value. For values themselves are implicitly defined here as possessing no material qualities.

The writing subject claims that institutions emerge to produce that which is ceded, ostensively serving the value that arises from that need. The first step in the institutionalization of values is demarcated at the point when the value purportedly served by an institution becomes confused with the product of the process specific to that institution. A value becomes fully institutionalized when the value ascribed to the product in the first step is transferred to the institution specific process of production. Because the value is now confused with the institutional process of production, the institution does not serve the originally authentic human value. Rather, the institution now serves the needs of its own processes, for they are now the locus of value. Concurrently, the institution does not fulfill an authentically human need; it merely stimulates a demand for its process of production. Moreover, when institutions fail to serve human values and, instead, serve institutional values, human beings are manipulated to become dependent on institutions.

In more specific terms, the concept of *learning* is formed in *Text Two* as an authentically human need. The concept of *education* is formed as an authentically human value that arises out of that need to learn. Within the context of the concept of *institution,* the school *qua* object is formed in this text as the site of a specific process of production. Because the value of education emerges out of the need to learn, the school surfaces to purportedly serve that value by fulfilling that need. What the school alleges to produce is learning; learning is formed within this institutional context as the product of the school's process. The school produces learning by means of processes of instruction. Neither the product of the school nor its process should be confused with the value of education. However, the value undergoes the first stage of institutionalization when it becomes confused with the learning that is produced by the school through its processes of instruction. The value of education is fully institutionalized when it is confused with the processes of instruction that are specific to the school.

Now that education *qua* value is equated with the school's processes of instruction, the school begins to function to maintain and reproduce these processes, for they are now the locus of the value served by the school. Moreover, the school fails to serve the human value of education. Instead, it serves the institutionalized value of education that is manifested in its own institutional processes. Concurrently, the human need to learn has been transformed into a consumer's demand for the school's instructional processes. Those processes *qua* institutional value, therefore, undergo a materialization of sorts. They are transformed into a commodity produced by the school *qua* factory.

The "myth of institutionalized values" is directly related to this text's formation of the school as church and the institutional processes of schooling as religion. The modern school system is constructed by the writing subject as serving three interrelated purposes that were once served by the Church. "It is simultaneously the repository of society's myth, the institutionalization of that myth's contradictions, and the locus of the ritual which reproduces and veils the disparities between myth and reality" (Illich, 1970b, p. 54). *En toto,* these three purposes or functions of schooling constitute the school as what the writing subject describes as the most "all encompassing…, dull, protracted, destructive, and expensive" ritual of initiation into social mythology that the world has ever known (Illich, 1970b, pp. 54-55).

In the analogy that is drawn here between the school and church, the school *qua* object is formed as a site of ritualistic initiation, while schooling qua concept is formed as the ritualistic process of initiating individuals into society's myths. As already witnessed in the previous discussion of the "myth of institutionalized values," the myths that schooling is said to initiate individuals into are constructed in *Text Two* as values which are conducive toward the maintenance and reproduction of a "consumer society."

The "myth of institutionalized values" is a vital myth for individuals to be initiated into. Once they have accepted this myth as reality, having rendered themselves dependent on and addicted to school for their learning, they can easily be made dependent on other institutions for the fulfillment of their consumer demands. This is the "myth of unending consumption." The need for school and the consumption of its product (schooling) establishes a pattern for future needs and future consumption. The need for the hospital leads individuals to consume that the institution defines as "health care." The need for General Motors leads individuals to consume automobiles. In all three instances, the primary discourse functions to form the relevant objects and concepts within the context of the "consumer society." In the transformation from the "human" to the "institutional," values and needs take on a material form that facilitates the notion of consumption as the primary activity of those suffering from "underdevelopment" and "modernized poverty." They cannot create the environment for themselves; they are initiated into a pattern of existence whereby they learn to simply consume the by-products of the institutions that do shape the environment.

As conceptualized in *Text Two*, the initiation of individuals into the myth of institutionalized values leads them to *equate* the value of education with the institutional processes of the school. These instructional processes have been transformed into a commodity. This facilitates a concomitant rite of initiation carried out by the school, an initiation into the "myth of measurable values." As a commodity, the value of education that is made manifest in the school's processes of instruction takes on the appearance of something that is material. Only that which can be conceptualized as a material entity is capable of being measured. In this context, the value of one's education can be measured by the number of years that she/he has spent consuming instruction.

This measurement of the value of one's education reflects the occurrence of another rite of initiation that the writing subject claims obligatory schooling forces individuals to pass through. The myth associated with this rite is the "myth of self-perpetuating progress." As pupils pass through the school system, they ascend to higher and higher levels of consumption. Those who measure the value of their education by the criteria of these levels conceive of the school system as a sort of ladder. The higher they climb, the more progress they perceive themselves as making. Whatever may be judged along the way that could be used as a criterion for judging one's education is secondary to the number of rungs that have been ascended during the years of instruction that have been accumulated and consumed. Thus, the value of one's education is judged in material terms.

The product of the instructional process (learning) is also conceptualized as a material entity. "School pretends to break learning up into subject 'matter,' to build into the pupil a curriculum made of these prefabricated blocks, to gauge the result on an international scale" (Illich, 1970b, p. 46). The institutionalization of learning as a need, then, involves a materialization, a segmentation, and a quantification. This threefold process is formed as a harbinger of a subsequent internalization. Once the individual accepts this institutionalized notion of learning, she/he can be made to judge her/himself in accordance with the scale of measurement set forth as "holy" by the school. Individuals, therefore, no longer need to be forcibly kept in their place in a stratified society. Schooling not only assigns them that place, it also induces them to accept it as a reflection of their "natural abilities" as measured by the school. Through internalizing this "measure" of themselves, these individuals learn to base their self-concepts upon the quantified value of themselves generated by the schools.

Those who accept this value are easily led to accept as valuable only those things that are measurable, and therefore only those things that are material. Such acceptance breeds underdevelopment and modernized poverty, for to think of methods by which one could shape her/his social world would be to employ one's powers. Creative thought, however, is threatening to those who are initiated into the "myth of the measurement of values," because it entails thinking in a fashion that extends beyond the conceptual boundaries of that which has already been measured and set forth as the material conditions of reality. It threatens to create deep fissures across the surface of the reified lens through which one receives the world, disrupting the comfortable numbness that can come with dependence. Taking the responsibility for engaging in creative action upon the social environment is even more threatening, because it would involve actively participating in the formation of practices to be pursued outside of the established situational frameworks upon which one had previously been dependent. It would mean actively giving shape to one's values, rather than passively accepting the pre-packaged models produced and distributed by institutions.

The "myth of prepackaged values" is the fourth myth formed here to support the conceptualization of society as a consumer society. School initiates individuals into this myth by distributing curriculum as "a bundle of planned meanings, a package of values, a commodity whose 'balanced appeal' makes it marketable to a sufficiently large number to justify the cost of production" (Illich, 1970b, p. 46).

Thus, curriculum is formed as a component of learning, the school's product. Though conceptualized as a component of the school's product, it is not presented here as being produced by the school. Teachers, as agents of the school, distribute curriculum, and pupils, as the clients of the school, consume it. But curriculum is formed in this statement as the product of "allegedly scientific research, on whose basis educational engineers predict future demands and tools for the assembly line, within the limits of budgets and taboos" (Illich, 1970b, p. 46).

Initiating individuals into the "myth of prepackaged values" plays a complementary role to their initiation into the myth of measurable values. The latter involves persuading them to accept their existence within a stratified society, the former molds them to meet the needs of the labor market. The labor market plays its own role in maintaining a stratified society. By initiating victuals into the myths of measurable and prepackaged values, the school functions to reproduce socio-economic classes.

But the curriculum that arrives at the school as an assemblage of prepackaged values does more than transform individuals into marketable values that can be fed into the labor market; it also persuades them to adopt marketable values. In Foucauldian terminology, as a mechanism of discursive regulation, the school initiates pupils into a worldview that is commensurable with social reality as received by those whose material interests are best served by the maintenance and reproduction of the present institutional arrangements and socio-economic relationships that characterize a consumer society.

Within each of the myths that are constructed in *Text Two*, something is conceptualized as a product that is consumed as individuals pass through the initiation rites of schooling. Initiation into the "myth of institutionalized values" induces them to consume instruction, indeed, to demand instruction from the school. This precipitates an initiation into the "myth of self-perpetuating progress." Because education *qua* value has become confused with the instruction provided by school, individuals ascribe value to their own education on the basis of the number of years that they have spent consuming instruction in school. This myth is very closely related to the "myth of measurable values," which convinces individuals to consume/internalize the measured value of themselves that is determined by the standards of the school. Initiation into this myth also persuades people to ascribe value only material things and to things which can be conceptualized in material terms, for only to material entities are measurable. The school initiates people into the "myth of prepackaged values" via the curriculum, for the curriculum itself is a set of prepackaged values that are to be consumed by pupils in order for them to become marketable values *qua* workers and in order for them (*qua* citizens) to adopt marketable values. Finally, by initiating individuals into the "myth of never-ending consumption," that school establishes the basis of a pattern whereby people will continue to consume any number of a wide variety of institutionalized values.

Both singularly and cumulatively, these myths are formed by the critical functionary in a manner which reinforces the conceptualization of society as a consumer society, a society of individuals who have been conditioned, in part, by the initiation rituals of obligatory schooling to consume. Because schooling is obligatory, the school has effectively established a *radical-monopoly* over the institutionalized and commodified value of education. This radical-monopoly guarantees that education which occurs outside of the school's authority of certification will be granted no currency. The value that is attributed to education as commodity is determined by its having been consumed within the institutional structure of the school.

According to the critical functionary, the human need for education has been transformed into a consumer's demand, and the consumers are dependent upon the school for its fulfillment. (It is important to recognize that there is a difference tween fulfilling a demand and satisfying a need. Individuals can have their demand for food that can be prepared and consumed quickly to meet the demands of their lifestyle fulfilled through the drive-through window at Hardee's, without having satisfied their need for nutrition and/or aesthetic pleasure.) It is in this sense that it is possible for the critical functionary to proclaim that society has been schooled, and the revolutionary functionary to proclaim that society must be deschooled.

The effects induced by the "schooling of society" arc described through the formation of two concepts. First, schooling produces a dependency on the school for the fulfillment of the public's demand for the commodity of education. This dependency stimulates underdevelopment. The formation of the concept of underdevelopment is based upon a particularly high value being attached to the individual and collective forms of participation in shaping the social environment. Underdevelopment refers to an undermining of the capacity to envision the occurrence of such participation. Reality is perceived through a reified lens. It becomes a matter of stripping individuals' power over their own social world. It becomes a matter of 'common sense" to view the school as the only valid place where individuals can have their demands for education met.

At the root of underdevelopment is the second concept that characterizes the effects of schooling. This is the concept of modernized poverty:

> The poor have always been socially powerless. [Modernized Poverty], the increasing reliance on institutional care, adds a new dimension to their helplessness: psychological impotence, the inability to fend for themselves. (Illich, 1970b, p. 11)

The modernization of poverty has led to a sterilization of individual and collective capacity for social initiative. The ensuing dependency on institutions of the welfare bureaucracy such as the school is experienced as a form of addiction. When framed within the context of addiction, the commodity that is demanded from school is formed as a treatment. The expectation that the poor hold toward this treatment is that it will lift the spell of economic poverty that has been cast upon them. In the public sphere, then, the school is formed as an institutional site that is similar to a clinic in its function and purpose. When the expectations of the poor are frustrated, when the desired results are not produced, and the poverty-stricken find their conditions are not being improved by the current treatment, the effects of modernized poverty and underdevelopment induce them to demand more and better treatment from the school. The apparent public consensus on the viability of this clinical treatment is evidenced by the amount of public funding that is spent on meeting these demands:

> Between 1965 and 1968 over three thousand million dollars were spent in U.S. schools to offset the disadvantages of about six million children. The programme is known as Title One. It is the most expensive compensatory programme ever attempted anywhere in education, yet no significant improvement can be detected in the learning of these 'disadvantaged' children. (Illich, 1970b, p. 12)

The conclusion drawn in this statement from the failure of Title One and all other programs to fulfill the demands and expectations of the poor is neither that not enough money was spent nor that the money was not spent competently. Rather, the conclusion is drawn that "educational disadvantage cannot be cured by relying on education within the school" (Illich, 1970b, p. 13). Moreover, while the education that is provided by the schools is formed in the public sphere as a treatment to be administered by the clinic, it is formed within this statement as a "snake oil" dispensed at a "medicine show."

As individuals become increasingly dependent on institutions for the satisfaction of their needs, greater demands are placed on those institutions. Concurrently, the reified view of reality that accompanies dependence generates a staggering degree of frustration among those who, while dependent on institutions, do not have the capacity to consume at higher levels of commodified values. Due to their reified view of reality, they themselves ascribe value to those commodities. And, due to their degree of dependence, they turn to institutions to assistance in developing the capacity to consume more freely. (Indeed, within this reified world view proper to a consumer society, freedom is defined as the freedom to consume as much of whatever one has a demand for.)

The inability of institutions to sufficiently contribute toward the poor's pursuit of their desired levels of consumption generates even more frustration. Nevertheless, the disenfranchised continually demand institutional solutions. But, as stated by the critical functionary, they have confused "salvation with the church." They have failed to recognize that the therapies offered by institutions are little more than snake oils.

That the school can administer enough treatment to alleviate the suffering experienced by the poor as the result of their educational disadvantages is a claim that is manifested here as illusory. The critical functionary presents these claims as forms of false advertising, charging that instead of contributing to the disestablishment of poverty, faith in the beneficence of obligatory public schooling intensifies the effects of modernized poverty. On the one hand, this belief strengthens the legitimacy of the school "as the institution which specializes in education...[and] discourages and disables the poor from taking control of their own learning" (Illich, 1970b, p. 15). On the other hand, it convinces the poor of their inferiority and, thereby, justifies their inferior socio-economic status and heightens their degree of underdevelopment. The polarizing effects that schooling has on society reveals its paradox: the more money that is spent on schooling, the more destructive it becomes.

Though powerful in their rhetorical role and poignant in their metaphorical use of language, the various formations of school *qua* object and *qua* concept present in this statement are only supplements to a more explicit construction. This formation is also more central in the amount of discourse that it generates than were previous formations. Here, school is formed as a concept. It is the conceptualization of a practice, as an age-specific, teacher-related process requiring full-time attendance at an obligatory curriculum" (Illich, 1970b, p. 32). Forming school in this fashion enables the critical function already at work here to operate at a deeper level by addressing the specific components developed within this concept of school.

First, individuals are sent to and grouped within school on the basis of their age. School is where children within the range of certain ages belong. School is where they learn, for that is the only place where they can be taught. Because they are so deeply ingrained into the collective consciousness of a schooled society such as our own, these three assumptions draw considerable attention from the critical functionary. The critical function operates upon these assumptions to first expose r historically contingent nature, for things have been and can be otherwise.

Mandatory public schooling is a modern phenomenon. The particular notion of childhood that dominates Western societies is also a modern phenomenon. Though little erudite explication is provided, the claim is made in this that schooling serves to mass produce childhood. The strong implication, however, is that the modern notion of childhood has been constructed as a category of individual whose moral, intellectual, psychological and/or physical immaturities prohibit her/him from being regarded as a responsible worker/citizen. Schooling, then, can be said to mass produce childhood in the sense that the number of years required for a child to attend school represents the length of time that the school needs to develop a responsible worker/citizen. Until the time requirements and the performance-based standards of the school are met, one or more aspects of the individual's maturity will be cast under the shadow of doubt:

> Institutional wisdom tells us that children need school, that children learn in school. But this institutional wisdom is the product of schools because common sense tells us that only children can be taught in school. Only by segregating human beings in the category of childhood could we ever get them to submit to the authority of a school teacher. (Illich, 1970b, p. 35)

The belief that the child's moral, intellectual, psychological and physical immaturities are best developed in the school serves to define the child as pupil. School is held to be the milieu of childhood. The second element of the definition of schooling that falls under the scrutinizing eye of the critical functionary is the idea that learning is teacher-related. In the context of the modern notion of childhood, learning, as a maturation process, is believed to be character-building. It is therefore officially certifiable only if it is the result of school teaching. This belief is contested in the critical functionary's formation of three arguments. First, most of the individual's learning occurs outside of school. Second, most of the concern toward schooling exhibited by parents is oriented toward the certificate that their children will be awarded and the amount of economic status it will enable them to acquire. Third, when and if children actually learn in school, it is the result of extrinsic motivations like those which stimulate the concern of their parents. It is not the result of superior teaching methods, neither is it the result of any intrinsic motivations developed within the student by the nature of school knowledge. Moreover, the good intentions of teachers have little impact on what individuals actually learn.

The third component of this explicit formation of schooling *qua* concept that the critical functionary operates on is the notion of full-time attendance. In the argument developed here, children are not formed as students, but rather citizens of the United States. This formation is then contrasted with the formation of the child as student performed by those who possess "institutional wisdom." This contrast is made in order to reveal a fundamental contradiction. Even though they are citizens of a nation state which claims to be a democracy, children are not afforded e*qua*l rights. The school recognizes neither the First nor the Fifth Amendment rights of the child *qua* student. In the case of the former Amendment, children are free to say whatever they wish. Textbook knowledge requires textbook answers to textbook questions. In the case of the latter Amendment, students are forced to undergo examinations. Examinations entail a form of questioning. Schooling does not afford children the right to refuse to participate in the examination, even though answering the questions may incriminate them as having failed to dedicate themselves to the program that the school has designed for them. Whether they participate in the exam or not, those who are not dedicated to the program are punished, and dedication begins with attendance. Both are obligatory.

The time and energies of teachers are also monopolized by the school. As is true of so many of the objects within this and other of the primary statements so far considered, the teacher is formed as a multiplicitous object. At once, she/he is custodian, moralist, and therapist. As custodians, teachers are required to lead their students through the rituals of schooling. As moralists, teachers inculcate wisdom in children that will teach them to distinguish between right and wrong. As therapist, the teacher's invasion of the student's personal life subjects the student to a "domestication of her/his vision of truth and her/his sense of what is right." Though these functions of the teacher overlap one another, it is important for them to be presented separately by the critical functionary in order to highlight the totalizing authority that teachers are expected to wield over students.

To this point, the treatment of *Text Two* has been concerned with the manner in which the school *qua* institution and schooling *qua* practice contribute to a life of consumption, dependence, underdevelopment, and modernized poverty. Moreover, the issues addressed by this theoretico-active analysis have thus far been confined to those which are relevant to the school as a manipulative institution. But this represents only the activities of the critical function which operates at the extreme right of the institutional spectrum. What has yet to be addressed is the revolutionary function that operates at the extreme left of this spectrum to generate the concept of the school as a convivial institution.

The mythologization of values and the frustrations of the poor that are generated by manipulative institutions do not provide the cultural revolutionary with a justification for doing away with institutions. The strategy of the revolutionary that functions in this and in previous statements is not to dissolve institutions, but rather to dissolve the dependence on institutions that characterizes a consumer society. This does not require getting rid of institutions. It does demand, however, that institutions be revolutionized. This institutional revolution is formed as part and parcel of a larger cultural revolution aimed at displacing the culture of consumerism. These complimentary revolutions are to be sparked by an awakened awareness among individuals of the futility of their dependence on institutions. This claim is substantiated by a number of discursive maneuvers performed by the critical functionary. First, in conceptualizing the school as an institution, the school *qua* object is formed as the site of a productive process. It is formed as a factory, as are all institutions within a consumer society. The productive process that is proper to modern schools is termed 'schooling.' Schooling is but the first process that individuals undergo as they are set upon an assembly line to be passed from institution to institution. Each institution has its own set of practices that are to be brought to bear on individuals, but, as the first site of production, the school is of particular importance to the later institutional processes. This importance is reflected in the formation of the school as a church, as the site of a ritual initiation into the myths/values that support the institutional structure of a consumer society. The school, therefore, is formed as the institution that is most responsible for the maintenance and reproduction of those institutional arrangements. By forming the school as an institution whose function of ritual initiation is so vital for the consumer society that is to be displaced, the critical functionary provides the cultural revolutionary with a target at which to direct the forces of change. The revolutionary function, then, forms the school as the linchpin of institutional and cultural revolution.

Again, unleashing the forces of institutional revolution on schools is not tantamount to a process aimed at eliminating them. That one of the central aims of this process is to transform the school from a manipulative institution to a convivial institution is testimony of this fact. Neither, however, is it a process aimed at the simple reformation of obligatory schooling and its curriculum in order that the schools would reflect a set of values antithetical to the goals of a consumer society. Such reforms would fail to address what is constituted as the central issue at stake here, which is *dependence*. To address this issue, the revolutionary function is not interested in reforming the school to become an institution that would itself serve a revolutionary function in society. Rather, the process by which society is to be revolutionized and the school is to be transformed is the process of *deschooling*.

The concept of deschooling is grounded in the earlier expression of education *qua* value, that it is an authentically human value that emerges from the authentically human need to learn. It should be recognized that it was on this basis that the critique of schooling as manipulation of this human need was formulated. In order that the school can function as a convivial institution, the value of education must be returned to its original condition of human authenticity; for this to occur, the authentic human need for learning must be protected from institutional manipulation. The formation of these conditions precipitates the call for laws which would enact both a separation of school and state and a prohibition of job discrimination on the basis of an individual's level of instructional/educational attainment. These same tactics that can protect "the need to learn" from manipulation also guard against the dependencies generated by obligatory schooling. A significant proportion of the justification for the separation of school and state is to prohibit the state from enacting any law which forces individuals to attend school. While this would effectively outlaw *de jure* obligatory schooling, the law concerning job discrimination is aimed at impeding the deployment of coercive powers which might lead to the establishment of *de facto* obligatory schooling.

In order for the school to serve as a convivial institution, the individual must be free to pursue education as an expression of her/his authentically human need to learn. As an object of the discourse generated by the revolutionary functionary, the school is formed as but one resource within a whole network of learning webs to which the individual may turn in pursuit of her/his self-defined educational goals. There is no need to explicate the specificities of these learning webs. It is important to point out that they should be formalized in such a manner that individuals are guaranteed *equal* access to them. It is also important to discuss the formation of the individual *qua* concept.

Again, the conceptualization of education as a value which stems from a need to learn is vital to a further conceptualization–this time, that of the individual. It is apparent that the individual is formed in this statement as the carrier of an internal drive to learn. That this drive should not be manipulated by an institution is posited here as a given. Therefore, the individual is constituted as a *self-directed learner,* and the proper function of the school as a convivial institution is a supportive one, one that supports the interests and activities of the self-directed learner rather than the interests and the processes of the manipulative institution. That the individual should be allowed such freedom as an active participant in her/his education is central to the formation of the concept of conviviality.

The concept of conviviality is formed in another text within the *oeuvre* as a principle of limitation. It is developed to demarcate the degree to which institutions can legitimately shape human activity and is linked to a particular notion of *austerity.* Contrary to our current association of austerity with the harshness of a Spartan existence, the concept of austerity is formed here as the foundational principle of friendship. It does not "exclude all enjoyments, but only those that are distracting from or destructive of personal relatedness" (Illich, 1973, p. v).

In that text, then, conviviality denotes an interest in the founding and the preservation of a sense of interrelatedness among individuals, while in *Text Two* conviviality is expressed as an interest in freedom of individual participation in shaping social experience and social reality. We can now expand upon the earlier contention that in order for the school to serve as a convivial institution, the individual must be free to pursue education as an expression of her/his authentically human need to learn. In contributing toward the individual's active participation in her/his own learning, the convivial school would be oriented toward maximizing her/his capacities as a self-directed learner. In its connections to the sense of austerity, however, the school *qua* convivial institution must not disrupt or distract from the individual's sense of interrelatedness with others. If possible, the convivial institution should even contribute toward this sense of personal relatedness.

The significance of this second criterion is most relevant for the role of the teacher in any formalized, yet convivial, institution of learning. The implications of this criterion can be drawn out by comparing the role of the teacher in a convivial institutional setting with the role of the secular minister described in a text not subjected to the method of theoretico-activism in this volume and the role of the culturally sensitive missionary described in yet another text not formally critiqued here.

In a series of other texts, a critical functionary is formed that is opposed to the church's active role in shaping social change (Illich, 1970a, pp. 95-106), the church's monopolization of religion (Illich, 1970a, pp. 69-94), and the church as an agency of cultural imperialism. On the basis of these criticisms, the revolutionary functionary moves to transform the role of the church. The transformation can be characterized here as a movement toward conviviality. After the transformation, the church is no longer formed as an active agency of social change and manipulation, but rather a nurturing mother of inward processes of development. No longer is the cleric a member of a professional elite who monopolizes religion within the institutional Church. She/he is transformed from a member of a manipulative institution into a member of a community. As a secular minister, she/he is formed as an individual who would be better informed of how the Church could benefit other members of the community. The same sort of transformation occurs between the culturally insensitive missionary who serves as an agent of a culturally imperialistic institutional Church and the culturally sensitive missionary who listens in the interest of silence and seeks meanings in the silence of syntony so as to adapt the Word of God to the culturally defined needs of the individuals whom she/he serves.

A similar transformation occurs here with regard to the teacher as an agent of the school. In her/his capacities as an agent of the manipulative school, the teacher is formed as custodian, moralist, therapist in her/his relationship to the pupil. In her/his relationship to the instructional processes of the schools, she/he is formed as a mere distributor of prepackaged values. Within the context of the school as a convivial institution, however, she/he is also formed as a member of a community who serves the human value of education in its authenticity. She/he perceives her/himself as serving the self-defined need to learn of the self-directed learner, who is also a community member. Their sense of personal relatedness to one another is strengthened by their shared experience of education as a value. It is within this framework that these individuals *qua* community members can be formed as participants in practices that are characteristic of convivial institutions.

In the comparison of the transformation of the teacher and the cleric from agents of manipulative institutions to agents of convivial institutions, we witness the formation of a partial unity between the texts analyzed here. There is a certain parallel between the treatment of the church and the treatment of the school. Both are subject to the effects of a critical function that operates in each of the statements which forms them as manipulative institutions which engender dependence, underdevelopment, and modernized poverty. The formation of these concepts serves the purposes of a revolutionary function, which is also at work in these texts. This function utilizes these concepts as contributions toward fostering the awakened awareness that is requisite to the revolutionary transformation of the institutions which breed them. Once these institutions are revolutionized, it is supposed that their dependence-inducing effects will be purged from society.

What separates this discursive practice from those within the archive of educational discourse, then, is its rejection of the pastoral image of the school as projected by those who advertise the school to be the mechanism by which either the individual or society can be elevated to a state of secular salvation in this world. It is through its rejection of this pastoral image of the school that this primary discourse violates the archive of educational discourse's messianic principle of inclusion. An individual who would appropriate this discourse as her/his own would stand a strong chance of rendering her/himself immune to both the school's and the church's exercise of pastoral power, for in so doing she/he would reject the notion that education and religion can only be gained within the school and the church, respectively. But in appropriating this discourse, she/he would not only situate her/himself outside of those institutions, but she/he would also leave her/himself vulnerable to being excluded from their respective archives of discourse.

In Chapter Four, I will describe how the messianic principle of inclusion that governs discursive practices within the archive of educational discourse is manifested in a series of commentaries which function to exclude the primary discourse from that archive.

References

Bowers, C.A. (1967). The messianic tradition in American education. *The Educational Forum*, 31:2, 203–209.

Brock, W. (1990). Will Americans work for $5 a day? *Time Magazine*, 23 July, 14.

Foucault, M. (1980a). *The history of sexuality, Volume I: An introduction*. New York, NY: Vintage Books.

Foucault, M. (1980b). Truth and power. In C. Gordon (Ed. & Trans.) *Power/knowledge: Selected interviews and other writings 1972-1977* (109–133). New York, NY: Vintage Books.

Foucault, M. (1982). The subject and power. In H. Dreyfus and P. Rabinow (Eds.) Michel Foucault: *Beyond structuralism and hermeneutics* (208–228). Chicago, IL: University of Chicago Press.

Illich, I. (1970a). *Celebration of awareness: A call for institutional revolution*. San Francisco, CA: Heyday Books.

Illich, I. (1970b). *Deschooling society*. New York, NY: Harper and Row.

Illich, I. (1973). *Tools for conviviality*. San Francisco, CA: Heyday Books.

CHAPTER FOUR

Practices of Exclusion

In Chapter One, I claimed that the significance of this work lies not in the elaboration of the primary discourse, but rather in the record that is provided of its exclusion from the broader field of educational discourse. Therefore, the reader should not expect to find in this chapter the construction of any arguments that I attempt to defend that primary discourse against its commentators, those who have been complicit in the practice of discursive exclusion. Again, I am more interested in demonstrating the manner in which their particular formulations of the principle of inclusion have been brought to bear against that discourse as principles of exclusion, banishing it from the archive of educational discourse.

Because the commentaries to be discussed here have been generated by different individuals, there is no concern for the theoretico-active suspension of the unity of any *oeuvre*. Because these commentators have their own distinctive ways of formulating the messianic principle that facilitate the inclusion of their individual discursive practices within the archive of educational discourse, the exclusionary forces which they have exerted upon the primary discourse cannot be described as monolithic.

Yet, this does not eliminate the possibility that unities between commentaries might be established on the basis of shared characteristics in their formation of the school as an object of discourse. In other words, the school can be formed as a messianic institution in a number of different ways, but unities can be established between discursive practices which are substantially similar in their formation of the school as a messianic institution. These observations are relevant to the degree that this chapter is divided into sections which correspond to the unities between commentaries. For example, the first section applies a theoretico-active analysis only to those commentaries which emerge from discursive practices that appropriate the messianic principle of inclusion to form the school as an institution that contributes toward a meritocratic society. These discourses conceptualize meritocracy as the realization of secular salvation.

Thus far, I have kept both the messianic principle of inclusion that regulates the archive of educational discourse and the rule of formation within the primary discourse which violates that principle at an abstract level. That is, I have not enunciated them in their specificity. I am obliged to do so before engaging in the ensuing analyses of discursive practices which conform to the messianic principle and the exclusionary forces that they exert on the primary discourse.

The messianic principle states that:

> In order for your discourse to enter the archive of educational discourse, the rules of formation that govern your discursive practice must constitute the school as a benevolent institution which can deliver either the single individual or society as a whole, or both, into a state of secular salvation.

The rule of formation that governs the primary discursive practice discussed in Chapter Three on the other hand, states that:

> The school, as an institution, is not capable of leading anyone to secular salvation. To the contrary, secular salvation can only be achieved if humanity abolishes its dependence on institutions such as the school for the fulfillment of authentically human values.

The remainder of this chapter is devoted to explaining how the discursive practices of a number of different commentators conform to the messianic principle of inclusion by determining both the nature of their respective pastoral images of the school and the contribution that this formation of the school makes toward the realization of their view of secular salvation. It will then be demonstrated how the commentators exercise this principal as a prohibition against the primary discourse.

Commentaries from Meritocrats

The first commentary to be subjected to theoretico-active analysis in this chapter activates the messianic principle of inclusion in the formation of a pastoral image portraying the modern school as a "potent conduit to social mobility" (Stanley, 1972, p. 51). Social mobility is to be understood as a liberation from systems of ascribed socio-economic status. The commentator, Manfred Stanley, conceptualizes the existence of certain special forms of knowledge. By forcibly exposing all individuals to these special forms of knowledge, mandatory public schooling provides everyone with the same opportunity to acquire what he refers to as "enabling functions."

Successfully learning these special forms of knowledge leads to the subsequent acquisition of the "enabling functions" associated with them. The successful learning of these forms of knowledge is conceptualized by Stanley as a process that requires moving through a series of sequential stages. Because the child may find nothing inherently interesting about the knowledge that she/he must engage in in order to procure the "enabling functions" that they present, she/he must be coerced into the sequential stages of learning that are embodied in the school.

Such coercion is justifiable if all children are to be granted equal educational opportunity, that is, equal access to the "enabling functions" of the sacred knowledge that the school submits as the key to social mobility. Failure to provide individuals with this opportunity early in their lives is tantamount to "disabling" them, because the nature of these special forms of knowledge is such that they require individuals to enter the school's sequential stages of learning at a very young age while their minds can still be molded. "From the standpoint of the mind, a wasted youth could be catastrophic for later life, certainly in the case of individuals who subsequently discover that they desire a professional level of attainment in the arts or sciences" (Stanley, 1972, p. 51). Thus, while the nature of these forms of knowledge is never explicitly stated, they are constituted in relation to the concept the "demands of professionalism."

The equal educational opportunity that is provided to all individuals who are "justifiably coerced" to attend school is not, however, tantamount to providing them with equal opportunity in terms of social mobility. Only those who successfully learn the required forms of knowledge that will imbue them with the "enabling functions"' are provided equal opportunity in these terms. The elite status they will achieve as the result of their being imbued with these "enabling functions" is a signification of the merit that they displayed in learning the forms of knowledge which meet the "demands of professionalism." Hence, the elite status of these professionals is arrived at democratically. Their peers who did not achieve such status had the same educational opportunity that these professional elites had but did not display the same degree of merit as they moved through the school's sequential stages of learning. Therefore, they are not rewarded with the same degree of opportunity in terms of social mobility.

The various levels of class structure in a stratified society are justified on the basis of the high degree of merit displayed by those at the top of the hierarchy and the low degree of merit displayed by those at the bottom. In other words, those at the top are there because they deserve to be, and those at the bottom are there because they deserve to be. One's position in the social hierarchy is a function of one's merit; the school provides everyone with an equal opportunity to display their merit. And meritorious performance in school is said to translate into a position among the elite within society. Such is the nature of the democratic elitism characteristic of a meritocracy.

Meritocrats like Stanley assume that societies have always been and always will be governed by an elite group. It is their contention, therefore, that a society's elite is justifiable only if they achieve that status as the result of their merit, which is to be determined on a democratic basis. The pastoral image of the school is formed by the meritocrat's appropriation of the messianic principle of inclusion and the subsequent transformation of that principle into the following rule of formation:

> It is only possible to speak of the school as an agency which provides everyone with an equal opportunity to display her/his merit in learning the forms of knowledge that can be applied to serve the interests of society as a whole, for only those who display such

> merit can be charged with the task of leading society into the future.

A failure to provide everyone with the same educational opportunity is conceptualized not only in terms of individual disability, but also in terms of disabling both the future intellectual life and the future economic and technological development of a society. "One wonders, for example, where Japan would be today if her modernizing elites had not had recourse to schools as an instrument of mobilization and resocialization" (Stanley, 1972, p. 51). Without mandatory public schooling/equal educational opportunity, the meritocrat believes society would regress into forms of ascribed elitism.

At the level of the individual, then, Stanley forms a pastoral image of the schools in which they offer people from the lower strata of society an opportunity to better their station, to rise to the ranks of the elite who already enjoy secular salvation in its highest form. Because the enabling functions that the knowledge passed on through the school offers to the individual are manifest in the demands of professionalism, it is only through their acquisition that the individual can attain her/his desired level of professional status. The successful acquisition of these functions, therefore, merits the individual her/his status as a professional. And because the acquisition of enabling functions involves passing through stages of learning that individuals may not find to be particularly interesting during their youth, coercing them to attend school is nevertheless justifiable on the grounds that it is in their own future best interests. Without the schools, there would be no institutional mechanism by which to democratically determine which individuals should direct the affairs of society.

At a societal level, a lack of professionals who are in command of some elite forms of knowledge would disable a civilization's capacity to "progress." Coercing individuals to attend school, therefore, is also justifiable on the grounds that it is in the future best interests of society. Although society, as described in this commentary, is constituted by a group of elites who determine what, when, where the individual is to learn, the democratic elitism that is facilitated by the formation of public schools within a meritocracy is argued to be far preferable over the forms of elitism that were displaced by that meritocracy. "Schooling has, after all, liberated people from a variety of rather confining forms of ascribed elitism" (Stanley, 1972, p. 52).

It is not difficult to recognize that Stanley's commentary is guided by the messianic principle, for the school is formed within this discourse as an institution which has liberated individuals from forms of ascribed elitism and has contributed to the realization of a particular form of secular salvation (meritocracy). Stanley brings the messianic principle to bear against the primary discourse by arguing that "in attacking the elitism of schooling (which in a meritocracy is defined as democratic elitism), [the primary discourse] seems almost disingenuous in not pointing out the possible elitism of [its] own orientations" (Stanley, 1972, p. 52).

He fears that a new form of ascribed elitism would arise out of the circumstances created by a radical deschooling of society and predicts that educational certification programs would become privatized by various federal agencies and multinational corporations as well as by militant organizations. His prediction is carried further to argue that the educational programs established by militant groups would be:

> fueled by the increasing fragmentation of the larger society as social enclaves become ever more involuted to people no longer being exposed to any integrative influences of the sort once provided, however ineptly, by the schools. Instead, people are even more trapped in their social classes and strata. They have been deprived of compulsory schooling which, by exposing people to new motivations and possibilities, often functioned as a potent conduit to social mobility. (Stanley, 1972, p. 52)

By offering individuals the opportunity to acquire the "enabling functions" inherent in forms of knowledge that meet the "demands of professionalism," the various coercions involved in forcing individuals to attend school are justifiable for meritocrats such as Stanley. It is in the democratic elitism within meritocracy itself that society, by overcoming ascribed forms of elitism, has achieved a high degree of secular salvation. And the school offers the individual a share of this salvation in its formation as a "potent conduit to social mobility." This captures the essence of the meritocratic version of the messianic principle of inclusion that licenses those who adopt it in forming their discursive practices to speak within the community of educational discourse.

Though it falls outside of the discursive boundaries of the meritocrat's rules of formation, we find a certain sympathy with Stanley's argument in Neil Postman's concern for the elitist tendencies of the primary discourse. Postman (1973) asserts that the poor have no great desire to deschool society; what the poor want is educational reform that will provide them with "better schools and better teachers, and control over both" (p. 144). An elitist voice is then formed by this commentary at a level within the primary discourse which replies that, 'The trouble with the poor is that they just don't know what's best for them" (Postman, 1973, p. 144).

Robert Manners expresses a more committed form of solidarity with Stanley's commentary. Not only does he cite Stanley's meritocratic critique of the primary discourse, but he also argues, in effect, that the school's positive contributions toward a meritocratic society are manifest in the number of experts that the schools have produced and the material comforts that their technologies have provided us. And, in echoing the concerns for elitism raised by both Stanley and Postman, Manners finds it relevant to ask if an individual who might adopt the primary discourse, which is "tainted by Tolstoyan aristocratic sentimentalism for Third World cultures of poverty untouched by materialistic bourgeois aspirations, had ever really bothered to ask [the poor in Latin America] for their ideas about the good life" (Manners, 1975, p. 659).

This concern for the forms of elitism that might emerge after society's deschooling process stimulates the meritocrat to silence the primary discourse. This is especially true in regard to statements formed by the rules governing primary discursive practices such as: "School has become the world religion of a modernized proletariat, and makes futile promises to the poor of the technological age" (Illich, 1970b, p. 18).

Moreover, the meritocrat's satisfaction with the degree of secular salvation that democratic elitism has provided society, and the material comforts that the technologies and institutions produced and operated by the professional elites have afforded the members of society justify mandatory schooling. The pastoral image of the school as a "potent conduit to social mobility" that is formed by the meritocrats' appropriation of the messianic principle of inclusion offers the individual a form of secular salvation that is already enjoyed by those elites who have earned their passage to that salvation. The key word here, of course, is "earned," for the elite status of those who already enjoy the benefits of secular salvation is only a sign of their merit, which is defined as the talents they displayed and effort they exerted in order to acquire the "enabling functions" required by the demands of professionalism. To do away with obligatory public schooling would elicit the rise of ascribed rather than democratic forms of elitism. It would "disable" society's majorities by denying them the opportunity to achieve secular salvation by demonstrating the degree of merit that is required to meet the admissions standards of society's corps of professional elites.

Commentaries from Social Reconstructionists

Though meritocrats and social reconstructionists have historically been at odds with one another in regard to which pastoral image of the school is the most viable, their disagreements have excluded neither of them from the archive of educational discourse. The meritocrat contends that the school has already "enabled" society to achieve a remarkable degree of secular salvation, while the social reconstructionist argues that the role of the school in the formation of that society is hardly a messianic one and that the current social situation is certainly no realization of secular salvation. Moreover, the meritocrat and the social reconstructionist simply disagree on what secular salvation should look like. The two of them align themselves, however, when the messianic principle of inclusion that governs each of their discursive practices is challenged by the primary discourse.

To the extent that the primary discourse promotes its own vision of social reconstruction, a vision that moves along the lines of conviviality, it is not surprising that other advocates of social reconstruction would constitute the group within the discursive field of education to take the primary discourse the most seriously. By and large, the commentators from the social reconstructionist camp express agreement with the criticisms leveled at the modern school within the primary discourse. They also appreciate the formation that the school takes in the primary discourse's account of a convivial society. But this is where the rules of formation that govern the discursive practices of the social reconstructionists force them to part company with the primary discourse.

At the most general level, the rule of formation which reflects the social reconstructionists' appropriation of the messianic principle of inclusion that allows their often "radical" discursive practices to gain admission to the archive of education discourse, however marginally, can be stated in the following terms:

> In order to properly speak of the school, one must conceptualize it as an agency in order to fulfill its proper mission, gives rise to increased awareness among individuals of the radical changes needed to occur within society in order for a truly egalitarian society to emerge, for only with such awareness individuals become "empowered" to enact those necessary changes.

This general rule of formation is most clearly reflected in Herbert Gintis' (1973) claim that the very "idea of liberating education…is made possible by emerging contradictions in the larger society" (p. 68). And, most especially, it is reflected in his further claim that "the correct immediate political goal [of the school] is the nurturing of individuals who [are] both liberated (i.e., demanding control over their lives and outlets for creative activities and relationships) and politically aware of the true nature of their misalignment within the larger society" (Gintis, 1973, p. 71). This same rule governs the formation of Arthur Pearl's (1973) declaration that "schools must go beyond merely raising the problems; instead they most begin to suggest real solutions" (p. 116).

This rule of formation gives rise to the critical function that operates within social reconstructionist discourse. It is the critical function which forms the current system of schooling as a process that supports the oppressive social practices at work within society and reproduces socio-economic inequalities. The social reconstructionists, therefore, challenge the legitimacy that the meritocrat ascribes to the notion of "democratic elitism." Furthermore, it is the critical function's formation of the current system of schooling that stimulates the social reconstructionists to call for a number of educational reform proposals of varying degrees of severity. Though disparate in nature, these reform proposals arise as reactions against the "oppressive" practices that characterize the modern school. The reconstructionists characterize these practices "oppressive" because they fail to reflect the sorts of practices that would emerge from the pastoral image of the school generated by social reconstructionist discourse. That is, the modern school fails to function in a capacity to bring about the degree of critical awareness among individuals that would lead to their active participation in the forms of social reconstruction necessary for the attainment of secular salvation. This is the essence of Pearl's (1973) contention that "the institutional school has not, of course, been relevant to producing a 'desirable world'; that is why it must be reformed" (p. 115).

For social reconstructionists like Pearl, "universal education is necessary and must be organized because the threats to [humanity's] existence are universal" (Pearl, 1973, p. 114). Though they differ in the specificity of their criticisms of the status quo and the role played by the modern school in its maintenance, there is a general agreement among the social reconstructionists that the school must be reformed to play an active role in the transformation of society.

Moreover, the social reconstructionists are committed to the transformation of the school. They are driven by a "faith" in their capacity to do so, as well as by a concomitant "faith" that such a transformation can effect the further transformation of society into a state of secular salvation by nurturing students to do "their own kind of critical learning...at higher and higher levels of complexity" (Greene, 1973, p. 135). Their commitment to bringing about secular salvation and their faith in the pastoral power of the school to do so is largely responsible for the emergence of the commentaries they direct toward the rule of formation governing the primary discourse. To claim that the school, as an institution, is not capable of leading anyone to secular salvation threatens to shake their faith in mandatory schooling as well as their identities as "radical educators."

Though they find the primary discourse's critique of the modern school to be insightful and valuable, their own rule of formation cannot allow them to accept the monolithic social role that it ascribes to the school. To do so would disallow the possibility of the internal transformation of the school that they have in mind. It is the social reconstructionist's rejection of the monolithic role of the school and concomitant desire to induce a form of internal transformation of the school to reconstruct society that leads Pearl (1973) to state that "schools offer a variety of experiences and interests and provide a place for increasing numbers of 'radical' teachers to function. . .True educational reform inside and outside schools is really possible, then, because the schools themselves do not have an already established or predetermined role [in society]" (pp. 113–114).

While Pearl recognizes that "it will not be easy to create schools with a democratically oriented leadership that *convinces* rather than *coerces* people to acknowledge the importance of education," he claims that "what we have come to regard as human rights can be guaranteed only within an institutional structure" (Pearl, 1973, pp. 113-114). In further defense of the necessity of maintaining an institutionalized system of mandatory schooling, albeit a radically transformed one, Herbert Gintis (1973) adds:

> The social relations of unalienated education must evolve from conscious cooperation and struggle among administrators, teachers, and students, although admittedly in a context of radically redistributed power among the three...The experience of both struggle and control prepares the student for a future of political activity in the factory and office. (p. 66)

The social reconstructionists find some irony in the notion that the name of the speaker of the primary discourse which seeks to disestablish mandatory schooling is known, by and large, only by individuals who have experienced many years of compulsory education. Pearl uses this irony to defend the idea that the schools are not the monolithic institutions that the primary discourse makes them to be. The space which allows the "official" mission of the school to be subverted by radical teachers is not built into the school by design, Pearl (1973) claims. The school is, in fact, capable of developing "intellectual opponents to injustice" because any time that "a group of inquiring youths are compelled to interact with each other, a percentage will begin to question the values and direction of their society" (p. 114). That the schools do, on however limited a basis, produce individuals who challenge the various forms of oppression that are perpetuated by status quo practices, both discursive and non-discursive/social, provides the social reconstructionists with testimony to the revolutionary potential that lies dormant within the school. It also provides them with a justification for their appropriation of the messianic principle of inclusion that governs their rules of formation. There is, of course, a direct parallel that they draw between the "revolutionary potential" that is witnessed through the school's production of "intellectual opponents to injustice" and the pastoral image of the school that is the product of their discursive practice.

The primary discourse's denial of the potential within mandatory schooling to bring about secular salvation inspires the emergence of the exclusionary forces that are directed against the primary discourse in the formation of these commentaries. The primary discourse's suggested abolition of mandatory schooling is found by the social reconstructionists to be intolerable in its transgression of the messianic sense of hope that characterizes the reform elements of their discursive practices. In defense of their own project, the social constructionists conceptualize the individual as one who, without the guidance of the radical teacher, is indisposed to learning anything that might threaten her/his reified world view. To do away with mandatory schooling, to deny the individual the opportunity to experience even one brief glimpse of the school's potential to serve as an agency of positive social transformation, would grant the individual a license to learn only from those forms of knowledge that support her/his reified world view. As Pearl (1973) states: "to learn [only] what one likes is to learn prejudices," (p. 115) which are conceptualized as the manifestations of reification.

Social reconstructionists, then, conceptualize those reified forms of knowledge/prejudices as falsehoods which do not reflect the "true" nature of reality or the "true" nature of the individual's position within that reality. Such a conceptualization of the forms of knowledge that individuals gravitate toward if left unattended by the "radical" teacher is a revolutionary system of mandatory schooling leads Pearl to claim that "education self-selected is no education...we have such education currently available to us (it comes to us on half a dozen simultaneous channels on television) and there we find Gresham's law of culture: it drives out good, and the frivolous outdraws the serious" (Pearl, 1973 p. 115).

In Chapter Three, I described the characteristics of pastoral power identified by Foucault. Here, in this account of the social reconstructionists' defense of their messianic principle of discursive formation, we witness the conceptualization of the ideal school through which pastoral power flows. It flows, in this instance, not in order to know the conscience of the individual, but rather her/his "true" position within social reality. In revealing her/his position within reality to the individual, the agent who exercises the pastoral power that flows through this idealized school also functions to reveal to the individual the true nature of the social reality in which she/he is embedded. Once the "radical" teacher exposes the individual to these truths," as painful as that exposure may be for the individual concerned, she/he can become liberated from her/his previously reified consciousness and begin to struggle to overcome her/his oppressed circumstances and the oppressed circumstances of others. The direction that this struggle is to take, of course, is in the direction of the transformation of society and the realization of secular salvation. Meaning to be ascribed to this form of secular salvation is a world that is free of injustice and oppression.

Left to their own volition in directing their education, individuals would move in an irresponsible direction. Only under the instruction of the "radical" teacher can the individual be educated to assume "true social responsibility." For reconstructionists, the forms of knowledge to be disseminated through the schools that will contribute toward the transformation of society in the direction of secular salvation must challenge the prejudices and reified world view that most people carry with them. No matter how painful these "truths" (e.g., the forms of knowledge advanced by the social reconstructionists) may be to some individuals, they must nevertheless be exposed to these sacred forms of social reconstructionist knowledge if the injustices of society are to be rectified.

The form of secular salvation formed within the discursive practices of the social reconstructionists has been described as a society that is free of all injustice and all oppression. In a very strong sense, the concept of "oppression" functions in a manner that is similar to the function that the concept of "elitism" plays in meritocratic discourse. The meritocrats were concerned with the new forms of elitism that might arise as the result of deschooling. The social reconstructionists are concerned with the new forms of oppression that might emerge if society were be deschooled. This concern is clearly expressed in the following statement from Pearl (1973): "Try to deinstitutionalize education as a symbol and the beginning of deinstitutionalization of everything else, and you reinstitute the law of the jungle, which quickly breaks down into a new set of oppressive institutions" (p. 116).

Simply stated, then, the social reconstructionists conceptualize deschooling as a non-solution. At the level of the individual, disestablishing mandatory schooling would not promote the sort of educational process whereby everyone would necessarily gain access to the forms of knowledge that would lead to the development of a level of consciousness requisite for transforming society in a positive direction. At the level of society, this lack of consciousness would render individuals susceptible to new, perhaps even more insidious, forms of oppression and injustice than they had been subjected to previously.

The social reconstructionists acknowledge the relevance of the criticisms directed toward the modern school by the primary discourse, while their commitment to the internal transformation of the school for the purposes of secular salvation enables their discursive practices to conform to the messianic principle of inclusion. It is this commitment which inspires the formation of these commentaries as exclusionary forces against that primary discourse for rejecting the revolutionary potential of mandatory schooling. While the primary discourse states that secular salvation can only be brought about as the result of deschooling, the social reconstructionist is devoted to the pastoral power that lies dormant within the school as a mechanism of individual liberation and social change. This devotion is reflected in Sumner M. Rosen's (1973) criticism that the primary discourse:

> ...dismisses all reforms of education as simply serving to adapt and thus preserve the existing structure of power and privilege...overlooks the necessity of making day-to-day struggles over proximate objectives a part of the larger, longer, and more difficult process; it ignores the fact that these struggles bring together the potential forces that alone can make basic change possible. Deschooling will not solve the major ills of our society. (p. 103)

Gintis (1973) contributes to the exclusion of the primary discourse by echoing these same sentiments in his declaration that:

> Deschooling will inevitably lead to social chaos, but probably not to a mass movement toward constructive social change...The only presently viable political strategy in education, and the precise negation of [the primary discourse], is what Rudi Deutchke terms 'the long march through the institutions,' involving localized

> struggles for what Andre Gorz calls 'nonreformist reforms,' i.e. reforms which sufficiently strengthen the power of the teacher vis-à-vis administrators, and students vis-à-vis teachers. (pp. 70-71)

Finally, the commentary produced by Maxine Greene (1973) reflects this same response to the primary discourse from the social reconstructionist camp when she says: "I do not believe that oppressiveness, and consumerism, and racism, and violence can be overcome through changes in personal consciousness divorced from institutional stances" (p. 103).

Each of the commentaries from which these statements emerge rejects the primary discourse's contention that secular salvation can only be achieved if humanity abolishes its dependence on institutions for the fulfillment of authentically human values. Each of these three commentaries, each of the commentaries generated by other social reconstructionists, and each of those commentaries generated by the meritocrats, therefore, represents an attempt to exclude that primary discourse from the archive of educational discourse. They all reject the primary discourse's most fundamental rule of formation, and they all seek to negate it.

Both the meritocrat and the social reconstructionist might ask, however, "Doesn't the very appearance of that primary discourse stand as an attempt to negate the rules of formation that govern our discursive practices? Doesn't it strive to silence our discourses?" One may be tempted to jump to the conclusion that the primary discourse does, in fact, appear as a negation of the entire archive of educational discourse, which can further explain its exclusion. To jump to this conclusion, however, is jumping too soon and in the wrong direction. In order to direct a more careful movement in the right direction, an important distinction needs to be made here between commentary and discourse. On the one hand, discourse is the general practice of language. It can appear in a variety of forms that are governed by a variety of rules. Discursive practices which conform to the same set of rules constitute discursive formations. What has already been determined from this theoretico-active analysis is that there are at least two discursive formations included within the archive of educational discourse. Each of these formations is governed by its own set of fundamental rules. The most fundamental rule defining the meritocrats' discursive formation states that:

> it is only possible to speak of the school as an agency which provides everyone with an equal opportunity to display her/his merit in learning the forms of knowledge that can be applied to serve the interests of society as a whole, for only those who display such merit will be charged with the task of leading society into the future.

The rule that governs the social reconstructionist's discursive formation states that:

> In order to properly speak of the school, one must conceptualize it as an agency that, in order to fulfill its proper mission, gives rise to an increased awareness among individuals of the radical changes that need to occur within society in order for a truly egalitarian society (secular salvation) to emerge, for only with such awareness can individuals become "empowered" to enact those necessary changes.

We have also determined from this theoretico-active analysis that the primary discourse is governed by its own rule of formation which states that:

> The school, as an institution, is not capable of leading anyone to secular salvation. To the contrary, secular salvation can only be achieved if humanity abolishes its dependence on institutions such as the school for the fulfillment of authentically human values.

The primary discourse stands, within this study, as its own discursive formation. (This is not to suggest that there is no unity between it and other discursive practices outside of this work which would constitute them as elements within the larger discursive formation of "deschooling.") It is not a commentary. It is, rather, a discourse that adheres to the rules of a larger discursive formation. Discursive formations precede commentaries, for the rules peculiar to a discursive formation shape commentaries. These rules help to determine the nature of the comments that are made concerning a discourse belonging to a discursive formation that is governed by a different set of rules.

While commentaries could certainly be developed from the rules that govern the primary discourse which would amount to specific attempts to negate the rules of formation governing the discursive practices of either the meritocrat or the social reconstructionist, the commentary itself does not represent a specific attempt to do so. The difficulty is one of the degree of incommensurability between rules of formation.

The rules of formation governing the discursive practices of the meritocrat are incommensurable with those which govern the discursive practices of the social reconstructionist, but not to the degree that the rules of formation governing the primary discourse are incommensurable with both. Essentially, the meritocrat argues that the schools have helped society to achieve a form of secular salvation never before known to humanity. The social reconstructionist argues that the "democratic elitism' that is justified in meritocratic discourse is incorrigible, and that the schools must undergo drastic transformation if society is to be purged of such forms of systematic oppression. Though they are incommensurable with one another, both of these discursive formations are admitted into the archive of educational discourse because they each conform to the messianic principle of inclusion which mandates that:

> In order for your discourse to enter the archive of educational discourse, the rules of formation that govern your discursive practice must constitute the school as a benevolent institution that can deliver either the single individual or society as a whole, or both, into a state of secular salvation.

The disparity in the degree to which the primary discourse's rules of formation are incommensurable with those of both the meritocrat and the social reconstructionist is only explicable in terms of its transgression of this principle. No discursive practice that fails to adopt this principle gains admission to the archive. Such practices are punished for their transgression with exclusion.

In the theoretico-active analysis of the commentaries developed by the meritocrats and the social reconstructionists, we have witnessed how commentary functions as a mechanism of discursive control. We have seen how they transform the messianic principle of inclusion into a penal code for exclusion in their efforts to restrain the primary discourse, to impede the circulation and consideration of its meanings, to avert its powers and its dangers.

The extent to which the powers and dangers inherent in commentaries as discourses that serve as mechanisms of discursive control have been successful in slicing the primary discourse and excluding it from the educational archive is not able of being proven in any empirical sense. To prove their success at a less-than-empirical level of validity, however, would require that I betray the anonymity that I have thus far afforded the primary discourse by divulging the name of its writing subject. To a large extent, of course, that anonymity has already been betrayed in the endnotes to Chapter Three. Even those who do not pay attention to endnotes may well have easily discerned the name of the subject who enunciated the primary discourse approximately forty years ago. Such recognition would have been contingent upon the reader's familiarity with the literature. Those sufficiently familiar with the literature would have easily been able to associate the concept of "deschooling" with the name Ivan Illich. Such is the power of the author-function.

Revealing Illich's name at this point is not problematic. In fact, it is necessary in order to make the point that I wish to make here. In order to see the validity of my thesis that Illich's discourse has been silenced and excluded from the archive of educational discourse, first consider the following set of statements:

> Few figures have burst so dramatically onto the American intellectual scene as Ivan Illich. Articles in *The Saturday Review* and the *New York Times Review of Books* have brought him to the attention of a wide and important audience. *Time* and other mass media publications have bestowed on him celebrity status. (Rosen, 1973, p. 85)

> There may well exist somewhere an educational body which, like its counterparts in politics and the arts, takes upon itself to name a Man the Year in Education. If so, it would likely be tempted to name Ivan Illich its man of the decade...In keeping with the personality the man, the Illich phenomenon has burst upon the world with the energy of a volcano or an earthquake. (Piviteau, 1984, p. 393)

Now, keeping these statements in mind, consider this anecdotal narrative. While I was at the American Educational Research Conference in Chicago in

1991, I attended a philosophy of education social hour. I was speaking with Dr. Jim Garrison, a philosopher at Virginia Tech, about my work and was pleasantly surprised that he took a good deal of interest in my idea of attempting to explain the messianic principle of inclusion that governs the archive of educational course has been used to exclude Illich's discourse from that archive. He was so interested, in fact, that he sought out and introduced me to Dr. Leonard Waks, who happened to have occupied the office next to Illich's at Penn State University. Dr. Garrison had me repeat to Dr. Waks that I had told him about my book. To this Dr. Waks replied:

> "Oh, really? That's funny, because whenever I'm out somewhere with him (Illich) and he meets someone new, they always seem to say, 'Oh yeah, I've heard of you. But I thought you were dead.'"

Again, this is hardly an empirical measure of the validity of my assertion that Illich's discourse has been silenced within the educational community, but I believe that it gets the point across. How could a person whose writings "burst" upon the education scene with such vitality have become so marginalized just twenty years later?

References

Bowers, C.A. (1967). The messianic tradition in American education. *The Educational Forum*, 31:2, 203–209.

Brock, W. (1990). Will Americans work for $5 a day? *Time Magazine*, 23 July, 14.

Foucault, M. (1980a). *The history of sexuality, Volume I: An introduction*. New York, NY: Vintage Books.

Foucault, M. (1980b). Truth and power. In C. Gordon (Ed. & Trans.) *Power/knowledge: Selected interviews and other writings 1972–1977* (109–133). New York, NY: Vintage Books.

Foucault, M. (1982). The subject and power. In H. Dreyfus and P. Rabinow (Eds.) Michel Foucault: *Beyond structuralism and hermeneutics* (208–228). Chicago, IL: University of Chicago Press.

Gintis, H. (1973). Toward a political economy of education: A radical critique of Ivan Illich's *Deschooling Society*. In A. Gartner, C. Greer, and F. Riessman (Eds.) *After deschooling what?* (29–76). New York: Harper & Row.

Greene, M. (1973). And it still is news. In A. Gartner, C. Greer, and F. Riessman (Eds.) *After deschooling what?* (120–136). New York: Harper & Row.

Illich, I. (1970a). *Celebration of awareness: A call for institutional revolution*. San Francisco, CA: Heyday Books.

Illich, I. (1970b). *Deschooling society*. New York, NY: Harper and Row.

Illich, I. (1973). *Tools for conviviality*. San Francisco, CA: Heyday Books.

Manners, R.A. (1975). Ivan Illich: Schooling and society," *Teachers College Record*, 76, 639–664.

Pearl, A. (1973). The case for schooling America. In A. Gartner, C. Greer, and F. Riessman (Eds.) *After deschooling what?* (105–118). New York: Harper & Row.

Piviteau, D.J. (1974). Illich: Enemy of schools or school systems? *School Review*, 82:3, 393–411.

Postman, N. (1973). My Ivan Illich problem. In A. Gartner, C. Greer, and F. Riessman (Eds.) *After deschooling what?* (137–143). New York: Harper & Row.

Rosen, S. (1973). Taking Illich seriously. In A. Gartner, C. Greer, and F. Riessman (Eds.) *After deschooling what?* (85–103). New York: Harper & Row.

Stanley, M. (1972). Illich defrocked. *Society*, 50–52.

CHAPTER 5

An Analogous Exclusion

THE TWOFOLD PURPOSE of this study has been to analyze the discourse of Ivan Illich and the commentaries that have led to his exclusion from the archive of educational discourse. The theoretico-active nature of this analysis has enabled me to determine the rules of formation governing Illich's discourse and those governing the discursive formations from which the commentaries emerge. Between the two texts from Illich that I formally subjected to theoretico-active analysis, I found a particular unity. Both of them are governed by a rule that denies the pastoral power of institutions to effect salvation, either spiritual or secular. Insofar as Illich was once a monsignor with the Catholic church and was once a major author within the discursive community of education, there is a certain analogy that can be drawn here. He has lost both of these statuses as the result of the above-mentioned rule that governs the formation of his discourse.

I have already described the forces responsible for his loss of stature as an author within the educational community. I would like to conclude this work by how he lost his ecclesiastical status as the result of the same rule that was responsible for the exclusion of his discourse from the discursive archive of education. In order to demonstrate this effectively, it is helpful to divide Illich's tenure with the church into three distinct periods.

New York

First, from 1952–1956, Illich was assigned to Incarnation parish in the New York Archdiocese. Though his experiences there were partially reflected in what was previously referred to in the third chapter as "*Text One*," it is useful to explicate that how text fits into biography.

Incarnation parish had been traditionally Irish in its ethnic composition, but that composition was undergoing rapid transformation because of a steady influx of Puerto Rican immigrants. This new population had created what was perceived as a problem for Cardinal Spellman and the entire New York archdiocese. As discussed in Chapter Three, the cultural forces exerted by the Puerto Rican church had not been capable of rendering the people dependent on its institutional forms for their sense of Catholicism. As a result, the Puerto Rican immigrants displayed no desire to come into regular and frequent contact with the institutional church in America. This lack of desire was interpreted as a lack of practice by the North American church, who sought a means by which such a desire could be induced among these new immigrants in order that they would come to view regular and frequent contact with the institutional church as a prerequisite for their spiritual salvation. Moreover, they were to be made to adopt a pastoral view of the institutional church.

In many respects, the intervention of the diplomatic functionary described in Chapter Three mirrored the role that Illich was to play in negotiating the relationship between the North American church and the Puerto Rican immigrants. In both instances, his intervention constituted a rejection of the pastoral image of the institutional church, a denial that an institution could guarantee spiritual salvation, and a transgression of the messianic principle that guided the formation of church doctrine and church practice. In other words, Illich denounced what he termed the church's "savior complex."

For Illich, the Puerto Ricans, in their unwillingness to reject their own culturally determined relationship to the church in the face of the cultural chauvinism displayed by the North American church, were not the source of the problem. It was the cultural chauvinism and "savior complex" of the North American church that was the problem. The issue for Illich was not to devise a method by which Puerto Ricans could be induced into giving up their cultural identity in favor of North American practices of Catholicism, but rather that the attitudes and practices of the North American church should display and effect more acceptance and understanding of the Puerto Ricans' culturally ingrained expectations of the role and function of the church in their lives. Moreover, Illich believed that the function of the church was to serve people, not the other way around.

To this end, Illich initiated many programs designed to increase the self-reliance of the Puerto Rican community without compromising their cultural identity. It was his idea that, because other ethnic groups in the United States celebrated their cultural heritage on particular days of the year, the Puerto Ricans should have their own feast day in recognition of their ethnicity and in honor of their customs. The first celebration of San Juan's Day was held on June 24, 1956, and Illich played a leadership role in organizing an outdoor fiesta in the quadrangle at Fordham University. The event was a greater success than most had predicted, attracting over 35,000 celebrants. He even managed to arrange for Cardinal Spellman to serve as the guest of honor. The success that Illich was having with the Puerto Rican population in Incarnation parish had deeply impressed the Cardinal, so much so, in fact, that Spellman made him the youngest Monsignor in the United States.

Puerto Rico

Illich's success in working with the Puerto Rican immigrants led to his reassignment to the Catholic University in Puerto Rico. His tenure there began in 1956 and came to an end in 1960. His commitment to serving the Puerto Rican immigrants in New York had necessitated his learning of the Puerto Rican vernacular of the Spanish language. This meant more than simply learning the sounds of the language and memorizing its grammatical rules; he would have to learn silences of the language as well. To accomplish this task, Illich not only immersed himself in the transplanted Puerto Rican culture which thrived on the streets of New York City, he also took what vacation time that he had to visit Puerto Rico. During these visits to the island, Illich was deeply disturbed to find that the North American missionaries in Puerto Rico were practicing a form of cultural imperialism which was parallel to the cultural chauvinism that the North American church had displayed in New York. The pattern which first surfaced in Incarnation parish reemerged, except here it is the North American church, as manifested in the figures of the missionaries, which was foreign. Rather than threatening the cultural identity of the Puerto Ricans with its chauvinism and savior complex at home, the North American church threatened that identity with its imperialism and accompanying savior complex abroad.

In fulfilling the responsibilities of his assignment to the Catholic University, Illich was to establish a training program for North American missionaries who were being sent to Latin America. Ostensibly, this simply involved providing them Spanish language courses. In creating the Institute for Intercultural Communication, however, Illich's top priority was purging the North American missionaries-in-training of their cultural superiority complex. The process of "de-Yankeefication" required the nurturing of cultural relativism and an initiation into the spirit of poverty. In contradistinction to the practices of cultural imperialism that Illich had seen from the missionaries at work in Puerto Rico, he believed that the missionary must be "willing to witness with his life, to a foreign people, the relativity of human convictions in front of the unique and absolute meaning of the Revelations" (du Plesix Grey, 1970, p. 249) Learning the sounds of a language alone, he argues, cannot bridge the cultural communication gap between two worlds. One must learn the silences of a language as well as its sounds. In order to get his students to listen to these silences of the Puerto Rican vernacular, Illich forced them to "live on simple native diets, inspired them to travel on foot and horseback to the wildest mountain regions in Puerto Rico, gave up his own punctuality to accustom them to the Latin sense of time, and grilled them with rigorous cross-examinations to get them to look at themselves and recognize their culturally defined contingencies."

The foundations for Illich's style of pedagogy at the Institute for Intercultural Communication are found in a chapter in *The Celebration of Awareness* (1970) entitled "The Eloquence of Silence." To describe these foundations, I will return to the language of theoretico-activism.

Firstly, there is a function developed within this article that can be characterized as a culturally diplomatic function. The diplomatic function stems from Illich's concern for the concept of cultural sensitivity, which is another discursive element developed here. As the diplomatic functionary who is at work within this text, Illich forms the concept of cultural sensitivity in relation to the concept of cultural imperialism. This concept is developed as the result of Illich inserting himself within the text as a critical functionary. The critical functionary's denigration of cultural imperialism and the diplomatic functionary's praise for cultural sensitivity are vital to the formation of the missionary as an object constructed by the discourse at hand.

Yet, there is a multiplicity of missionaries formed as the objects of the discursive practice manifested in "The Silence of Syntony." Formed as representatives of the institutional church, culturally insensitive missionaries operate within foreign communities as the agents of cultural imperialism and, therefore, underdevelopment. As a transitory formation in the discursive practice of transforming the missionary into a discursive entity imbued with the spirit of cultural sensitivity, a second missionary *qua* object is generated here. This missionary is formed in a more general fashion as a *listener* and a *speaker*. The culturally sensitive missionary that is formed here is incapable of speaking with relevance to the individuals she/he is to serve until she/he learns to listen to them properly.

The missionary *qua* listener/speaker is formed here on the basis of the concept of language. Language is conceptualized as communicating much more than words; it communicates meaning. The meanings communicated through language are cultural meanings. They reflect the manner in which a people make sense of their experience. Words are carried across by the sounds of a language; meanings are embedded within its silences. "It takes more time and effort to learn the silences of a people than to learn its sounds" (Illich, 1970, p. 46).

But the concept of silence is also multiplicitous in this text. The concept of silence just described is formed in direct relation to the concept of language as one of its constituent elements. There is, on the other hand, a whole taxonomy of silences that are formed in relation to the act of learning a foreign language. These silences characterize the relationship between the listener/speaker and the silences embedded within language.

First, there is *the silence of deep interest* that is characteristic of the listener/speaker who is culturally sensitive. This silence, even in its passivity, is an expression of love. The greater the cultural distance between the listener's world and the foreign world in which she/he finds her/himself, the more this silence expresses love, for there is a positive correlation between the degree of cultural distance between the world of the language acquirer and the world of the native speaker and the degree of difficulty confronting the non-native in closing this gap.

The silence of interest directly relates to the concept of a second silence–*the silence of syntony.* The syntony embraced by this silence is that which exists between that which is spoken and that which is experienced. The silence of interest is conceptualized in reference to the listening half of the transitory object in this text. The silence of syntony is conceptualized in reference to 'the speaking half of that object. The former is concerned with achieving an understanding of the experience of others. The latter is concerned with establishing an understanding in others, with making that which is spoken relevant to the manner in which they experience social reality. The capacity to establish the silence of syntony is contingent on one's ability to effectively engage in the silence of interest.

Only when one is capable of these two silences is she/he able to establish the third silence on the positive side of this taxonomy – *the silence beyond words.* This silence is conceptualized in reference to the personal relationship between the listener/speaker and those whom she/he attempts to understand through her/his listening and with whom she/he attempts to establish syntony through her/his speaking. In the silence beyond words, the listener/speaker has lost her/his foreignness to the community, which was once so culturally distant from her/his own. In this silence, there is a certain comfort and tranquility, for the formerly foreign listener/speaker has rendered her/himself familiar to those with whom she/he resides. These are the silences of the new missionary, the missionary who seeks to make the church and "her" message relevant to the development and experience of those she serves.

The culturally insensitive missionary, on the other hand, is incapable of learning the meanings within the silences of a language. Rather than listening in the silence of interest, this missionary listens in the *silence of indifference,* "which assumes that there is nothing I want or can receive through the communication of the other" (Illich, 1970, p. 46). Her/his cultural insensitivity is manifest in the silence alone. For her/him, the sounds of a language are amenable to an aggressive mastery of lexical definitions and grammatical rules. When she/he speaks, then, there is no concern for syntony. There is no desire to make that which is spoken bear any relevance to the cultural understandings of the people with whom one establishes verbal contact. Though one's own perception of the situation may be otherwise, the reality of these circumstances is that she/he is not communicating *with* others, but rather *at* them. Such is the nature of the second silence of the culturally insensitive – the silence of brewing aggression.

As opposed to the words formed from the silence of syntony, words formed from the silence of aggression "divide rather than bring together" (Illich, 1970, p. 48). Therefore, the words of the missionary who listens in the silence of indifference and who speaks from the silence of aggression will always be foreign to those with whom she/he resides. And the silence between the indifferent and aggressive listener/speaker will never be more than a silence of hell. Because she/he is deaf to the meanings that a people attach to their experience, the culturally insensitive missionary is incapable of serving those people. She/he would expect them to conform to the standards and norms of the institutional church that has been imported into their culture. Therefore, she/he could be properly accused of engendering underdevelopment, which is the essence of hell on earth.

Once again, Illich creates an interventionist function through his discourse that mirrors his role as a cleric. In establishing the Institute for Intercultural Communication, Illich sought to block the pastoral power of the church by transforming missionaries from servants of the church (agents of its pastoral power) into servants of the people. Such a transformation could only be brought about if the missionaries could learn to listen to the people in order to determine their self-defined needs, instead of telling them what their needs are as defined by the institutional church.

Illich is as stringently opposed to any involvement of the institutional church in a people's secular affairs as he is against the church's cultural chauvinism and imperialism. While in Puerto Rico, Illich was appalled by the Bishop of Ponce's reaction to the initiation of a government-sponsored birth control program. Bishop McManus formed a Catholic political party to run against Munoz Marin, the incumbent President whose administration had started this program, in the elections 1960. McManus had threatened the Catholic population with the excommunication of any Catholic who supported Marin's campaign for reelection.

In response to these circumstances, Illich wrote the "The Powerless Church," (1970) which deals with the theme of the proper role of the church in affairs. Because of the magnitude of the church's power, many groups have lobbied and continue to lobby for its alliance with their specific causes. Why would Illich, as a critical functionary, be opposed to the participation of the institutional church in social change? The answer to this question is found in the formation of the very concept of social change, the concept of development, and the formation of a second type of church *qua* object. In turning to the rules governing the formation of this church, it is essential to address the concept of development.

The concept of underdevelopment that was explained in Chapter Three was formed in terms of individuals being rendered dependent upon institutions for their sense of values and for the satisfaction of their needs. In this type of relationship, those values and needs are determined by the institution for the maintenance and future benefit of the institution. In this relationship, it is the institution which develops; it is the institution which is the active partner in its production and distribution of values and needs. Individuals are rendered impotent; they become merely the passive consumers of institutional values and institutional needs. As development in the institutional sense occurs in a seemingly endless fashion in the external, material world, the internal, spiritual development of the individual is increasingly stunted. They become less and less capable of experiencing their own development; and, thus, their efficacy in conceiving and initiating social change decreases. As their view of the world is increasingly reified, their potency in affecting change within their own social environment undergoes a gradual sterilization.

It is within this context that Illich, as a counter-researcher, reformulates the notion of development from its modern, institutional conceptualization as an outwardly directed material process to a more humanistic concept as an inwardly-directed, educational and spiritual process. Formulated institutionally, the concept of development is directly linked to underdevelopment. Formulated humanistically, development is a continual process of awakening awareness.

Though the concept of social change is distinct from the humanistic conceptualization of development, it is not the equivalent of institutionally-defined development, either. Institutional growth can certainly generate social change, but the development of individual and collective awareness can produce change as well. The former, however, occurs at the cost of humanistic development, while the latter occurs as the result of humanistic development. In either case, the concept of social change is formulated as a process that always involves a triple reaction:

1. The reorganization of social structure, which is felt as either subversion or revolution.
2. The attempt to get beyond illusions which justify structures, which implies the ridicule of ideologies and is felt as ungodliness or education.
3. The emergence of a new "social character," which is experienced by many with confusion and anguish (Illich, 1970, p. 101).

When brought about by the forces exerted by institutions, social change impedes human development. Therefore, "the moment has come for the church to withdraw from specific social initiatives-taken in the name of church structure" (Illich, 1970, p. 101). The Church, as formulated here, however, is not only an institution, but also a nurturing female figure – a "*mater et magistra.*" Often referred to in this text as "she," this nurturing mother is disassociated from social change but is cast as a leading actress in the process of development.

While institutional development is judged in accordance with the criteria of efficiency, material comfort, and affluence, the humanistic concept of development formulated by the cultural revolutionary is judged against human experience. "And this experience is not available through the study of tables but through the celebration of shared experience: dialogue, controversy, play, poetry– in short, through self-realization in creative leisure" (Illich, 1970, p. 99). Therefore, these forms of outwardly expressed internal impressions of lived experience are open to the influence of the church as an agency of meaning. The meanings which "she" is capable of inducing in individuals' impressions of experience are conducive toward the recognition of "the presence of Christ in the growing mutual relatedness that is produced through development" (Ibid). She can awaken individuals' awareness of dependencies and self-alienation. She "does not orient change, or teach how to react to it" (Illich, 1970, p. 100). She does, however, in effect, provide a Christian framework through which to interpret experience. "She challenges us to deeper poverty instead of security in [material. Or personally ambitious] achievements; personalization of love (chastity) instead of depersonalization by idolatry, faith in the other rather than prediction" (Illich, 1970, p. 100).

The strategy of the counter-researcher, in generating this new object (the church as "she"), is to define a role for the church that will make positive contributions to the concept of humanistic development. This role would replace the active role that the institutional church has historically played in social change is fostered underdevelopment The responsibility for social change is to be passed over to the secular religions of cultural revolutionaries, who also have an interest in the notion of an inwardly directed form of personal development.

Leaving the language of theoretico-activism and returning once again to the biographical account of Illich's role within the church, when Cardinal Spellman, who was on official church business in Puerto Rico, attended a luncheon with President Marin, McManus again threatened that any Catholic who attended this luncheon would be excommunicated. Upon learning that Monsignor Illich had violated this dictum, McManus ordered him to leave the island.

Cuernavaca

After months of searching for an appropriate site for the continuation of his missionary training program, Illich settled in Cuernavaca, Mexico, and established The Centre for Intercultural Documentation (ClDOC) in 1961. The need for such a program was, in Illich's mind, greater than ever, for in 1960, the Vatican decreed that in ten years the North American church would send 10% of its personnel to Latin America. Illich interpreted this move as a sign that "the church as It" was attempting to extend its institutional control over what it considered to be its territory. In effect, the North American church was being ordered to send its missionaries to begin shaping the Latin American church more in its own image. It also happened that the timing of this papal order coincided with the initiation of the Alliance for Progress, which aimed its forces of modernization toward the economic and technological development of Latin America. Taken together, these two programs signified, for Illich, an economic and political strategy against the spread of Castro-communism in the region:

> Upon the opening of our centre, I stated two of the purposes of our undertaking. The first was to help diminish the damage threatened

> by the papal order. Through our educational programme for missionaries we intended to challenge them to face reality and either refuse their assignments (to Latin America) or, if they accepted, to be a little bit less unprepared. Secondly, we wanted to gather sufficient influence among the decision-making bodies of mission-sponsoring agencies to dissuade them from implementing the plan. (Illich, 1970, p. 54)

To prepare those who were to accept their assignments, Illich put them through the same sort of missionary training that he had undertaken in Puerto Rico. In his attempt to convince as many individuals as possible not to accept their, he published essays such as "The Seamy Side of Charity" (1970).

Once again, as he did in "Foreigners, Yet Not Foreign," which was referred to in Chapter Three as '*Text One*,' Illich speaks of the North American church. In the context of "The Seamy Side of Charity," however, one primary relation of great importance has been reversed. It is no longer a people who arrives in a foreign land with particular culturally-ingrained attitudes and behaviors that deviate from the norms appropriate to and the expectations of the institutional church. Rather, it is the North American church and its agents that arrive in a foreign land ready to impose their norms and their expectations on peoples whose cultures are inappropriate for such institutional relations. Just as in Puerto Rico, these Latin American peoples were not dependent on the institutional church for their sense of Catholicism. Up until the 1960s, the Latin American church operated on the most meager of budgets. It could not support a large clergy.

Consequently, Latin Americans, being dispersed across the countryside, had little direct contact with the institutional church and its agents. In 1960, as mentioned earlier, all North American religious superiors within the Catholic church were directed by Pope John XXIII to send 10% of their priests and nuns to Latin America for the purpose of modernizing the Latin American church. The support of this large number of clergy (approximately 23,000) would require, of course, a large amount of foreign money. Much of the funding was to come from the coffers of the North American and the European churches and from the charitable donations of individual parishioners within these more privileged countries. A second and more grandiose reserve of money was a coalition of secular institutions who were partners with the North American church in the larger Alliance for Progress. Dominant among those institutions were a variety of political and economic interests concerned with the future of their neo-colonial empire in Latin America. In the face of Castro-communism and the threat that it posed to the status quo of the region, these interests within the Alliance for Progress realized that the security of future practices of economic imperialism were contingent upon strengthening the forces of cultural imperialism. Hence, "the Latin American church flower[ed] anew returning to what the Conquest had stamped her: a colonial plant that blooms because of foreign cultivation" (Illich, 1970, p. 60).

As described within the context of Chapter Three, the North American church is capable of breeding its requisite dependence among parishioners only if it has access to their bodies. Cultivating this dependency in Latin America, therefore, required an expanded number of missionaries, which explains the papal edict. Increasing the number of missioners would, in theory, increase the demand among Latin Americans for the institutional church in order to achieve their self-identity as Catholics. While forces within their cultures had previously shaped their relationship with the church in such a manner that was commensurable with the patterns of their cultures, external forces were now being exerted in order to transform that relationship:

> Massive indiscriminate importation of clergy helps the ecclesiastical bureaucracy survive in its own colony, which every day becomes more foreign and more comfortable. This imagination helps to transform the old-style hacienda of God (on which the people were only squatters) into the Lord's supermarket, with catechisms, liturgy, and other means of grace heavily in stock. It makes contented consumers out of vegetating-peasants, and demanding clients out of former devotees. (Illich, 1970, p. 62).

Commodified rituals, however, were not the only goods that the North American church was distributing through the Latin American church. "Men and money sent with missionary motivation carry a foreign Christian image, a foreign pastoral approach, and a foreign political message. They also bear the mark of North American capitalism" (Illich, 1970, p. 58).

As cultural imperialists, missionaries function as the handmaidens of economic imperialism and political subjugation. Within the context of the Alliance for Progress, Latin American cultures and societies are framed as being "underdeveloped." Those who appear to be so magnanimously concerned with the conditions of life in Latin America, then, take it upon themselves to export people and ideas that will contribute toward the development and the progress of region. "Progress," of course, is a normative construct. Therefore, the supposed charity of the North American church and the Alliance for Progress masks a hidden imposition of North American values on Latin American culture.

In a culture that has a limited supply of material goods, such as those in most of Latin America, it is unlikely that the values of that culture will be materialistically oriented. Because the North American concept of "progress" is derived from materialistic values, transforming the Latin Americans' value for religion from a spiritual value to a material value would represent a marked sign of progress. Once transformed, the Latin Americans' fulfillment of that value could only be accomplished through contact with the institutional church in its role as a distribution center similar to the earlier description of the school. It is in this fashion that their dependency upon the church could be generated. Once the dual transformation of religion as a value and the relationship between the institution and the people has been accomplished, the church could become a more viable center for distributing other North American values to Latin American peoples. The missionary's potential as an agent of the cultural imperialism requisite to the maintenance of economic imperialism would then become realized.

Like the texts discussed earlier, "The Seamy Side of Charity" contains a diplomatic function. Any individual who might speak this discourse would occupy a certain discursive space between an institution, in this case the church, and a people and their culture. In this capacity, Illich's strategy is to call to the attention of potential missionaries and potential philanthropists alike not only the incommensurabilities between the values inherent in Latin American culture and North American culture, but also the hidden economic and political agenda implicit in the papal edict. This strategy aims towards dissuading potential missionaries from accepting any possible reassignment and to potential philanthropists from contributing money to a cause that threatens the human values specific to Latin American culture.

While the messianic principle at work in the discursive community of education has functioned as a block to rigorous analysis and allowed many proposals to pass on sheer emotional appeal, Illich claims that the "savior complex" of the church has relied on an impulse supported by uncritical imagination and sentimental judgments" (Illich, 1970, p. 57). In stimulating this impulse, the church's exercise of its modern form of pastoral power in its participation in social change and development is legitimated. But Illich, in pointing out the discrepancies between the self-projected image of the church as an agency of secular salvation and the actual effects that it produces, rejects the pastoral power of the church *qua* institution to bring about salvation both in this world and the next. Thus, once again, Illich transgresses a messianic principle. And, once again, the consequences were forthcoming.

As Illich continued to transgress the messianic principle of ecclesiastical inclusion, his own position within the church came under fire from many quarters of the church's institutional hierarchy, particularly that of the Mexican church. Aside from its geographical location, Cuernavaca, as a site for the establishment of CIDOC, offered the additional advantage to Illich of being presided over by Bishop Mendez Arceo, who shared many of Illich's convictions. Though CIDOC was to receive the official support of Cardinal Spellman, Fordham University, and the American Bishops Committee on Latin America, the Mexican church abhorred Illich's activities at Cuernavaca. Long known for propagating the most reactionary brand of Catholicism in Latin America, the Mexican Church had been highly critical of and threatening toward Bishop Arceo even prior to Illich's arrival. The efforts of this hierarchy to dispose of Arceo increased with the coming of Monsignor Illich. It became a priority to rid themselves of both.

Seven years after CIDOC opened, Monsignor Illich was called to the Vatican. He was to respond to an official inquiry of his Christian faith. The eighty-five questions to which he was to respond were divided into four categories: "Dangerous Doctrinal Opinions"; "Erroneous Ideas Against the Church"; "Bizarre Conceptions About the Clergy"; and "Subversive Interpretations Concerning the Liturgy and Ecclesiastical Discipline." Illich's meeting in Rome with his inquisitors lasted little more than two hours. He refused to take an oath of secrecy; and he refused to answer any questions until he had been delivered a written copy of all of the charges being levelled against him.

Illich found that the questionnaire that he was presented with formulated "some of the questions in such a way as to apparently call on me, priest and friend, to implicate or accuse friends and confreres, indeed even the bishop of the diocese in which I live and work"; did not provide "any assurance of a fair hearing or basis for the development of my own defense"; and "made it *a priori* impossible for me to express (or for any judge to grasp) my real thought and the real meaning of my personality as a Christian and of my faith" (Illich, 1969, p.188). Illich believed that to answer questions of this nature, to participate, even if as the accused, in such an inquisition, would only diminish the splendor of the church.

Once this document was delivered to him, he sat at a small restaurant and composed his letter of resignation from the church.

Illich's refusal to recognize the messianic principle that governs modern institutions had, therefore, led to his exclusion from two communities. The ecclesiastical community is governed by a messianic principle which states that "it is only through regular and frequent contact with the institutional agents and practices of the church that one can be guaranteed spiritual and/or secular salvation." I have described a number of Illich's texts and actions which have challenged this principle in his exclusion from the clergy of the Catholic Church. However, Illich was driven out by forces that are exterior to discourse. These were the forces of the church *qua* institution.

The discursive community of education is governed by a messianic principle which states that: "In order to be guaranteed secular salvation, one must establish regular and frequent contact with the school in receiving one's education." In this instance, the forces of commentary have driven his discursive practices outside of the archive of educational discourse.

As evidenced in this double-exclusion, for individuals who believe in the pastoral power of institutions to effect salvation, the transgressions that are brought to life through lllich's voice are intolerable. Hence, Illich has not been heard from within the archive of educational discourse for many years. Presumably, he has not been heard from within the church for many years either. Perhaps Illich's exclusions prove his own point concerning the degree to which we, as a people who are subject to cultural forces, are dependent on institutions, and how intolerant we are when our comfortable dependence on institutions is called into question.

References

du Plesix Gray, F. (1970). *Divine disobedience.* New York, NY: Alfred A. Knopf.

Illich, I. (1969). Monsignor Illich's letter to Cardinal Seper. *America,* 120, 188.

Illich, I. (1970). *Celebration of awareness: A call for institutional revolution.* San Francisco, CA: Heyday Books.

CHAPTER SIX

The Archive and Other Transgressions

In the final analysis, the thesis of this book is that Ivan Illich's exclusion from the archive of educational discourse is most directly attributable to his violation of the messianic principle of inclusion. This principle determines which discourses are and which discourses are not to be included within the archive. In other words, it determines what can be said and what cannot be said within educational discourse. Illich's transgression of this principle may not be the only factor that has contributed toward his exclusion, but it is the primary reason that his discourse receives so little consideration within contemporary educational circles.

While it is impossible to prove this thesis on the basis of any empirical evidence, other transgressive voices can be identified as having been silenced for violating this same messianic principle. It is also possible to demonstrate that this principle does, in fact, govern educational discourse. Establishing the existence of the archive and determining its boundaries is not only possible, it is requisite to substantiating the viability of the thesis that I have put forward in this work. The purpose of this sixth and final chapter, then, is twofold. First, it provides this project with a greater level of specificity in developing the reader's understanding of the archive of educational discourse by determining the nature of the discourses that are included within it and by identifying some general characteristics of the speaking subjects who produce those discourses. Second, it provides examples of other subjects whose discursive practices, like Illich's, have been held in violation of the messianic principle of inclusion and have subsequently been excluded from that same archive.

The Archive

Discursive subjects who have been granted admission into the archive of educational discourse are those who engage in discursive practices which have and continue to be concerned with the establishment, the maintenance, and/or the reformation of mandatory schooling as a social practice. Though, as a group, these discursive subjects project conflicting pastoral images of the school and divergent visions of what constitutes secular salvation, a unity can be identified between them on the basis of their unquestioning allegiance to some form of mandatory schooling.

I've already demonstrated in Chapter Four how one group, the meritocrats, are inclined to silence discourses such as Illich's, because these sorts of transgressions threaten to disestablish not only the social practices performed by the school that sort and select individuals on the basis of their supposed merit, but because they threaten the very existence of the sorting mechanism itself. The second group that was identified as having registered the greatest number of commentaries against Illich's discourse, the social reconstructionists, are vehemently opposed to the school serving the role of a sorting mechanism which reproduces a society that is stratified along the lines of socio-economic class. But they are not opposed to mandatory schooling.

While they do not share the meritocrat's notion that mandatory schooling, in contributing toward the justifiable phenomenon of democratic elitism, has helped to establish a significant degree of secular salvation, the social reconstructionists envision the transformation of mandatory schooling as a practice that can generate the social forces requisite to the elimination of all forms of oppression. In their eyes, the democratic elitism that the meritocrats cherish as a pastoral function of mandatory schooling is, itself, a form of oppression (social reproduction) that can only be eliminated with the transformation of the school. Therefore, though they have a significantly different view of what constitutes secular salvation, the social reconstructionists are equally inclined to silence voices that reject the pastoral power which they view as a latent characteristic of mandatory schooling. Through the transformation of the school, they hope to make that pastoral power manifest.

A further unity can be established between the discursive subjects who have been granted admission into the archive of educational discourse on the basis of the common social space from which they speak. As a general rule, these discursive subjects are either faculty members in institutions of higher education, or staff members of private organizations or government agencies that are directly concerned with the regulation of schools and the formation of school policies. Recognizing this unity, one could easily develop a crass economic argument to the effect of: "Of course, these individuals are interested in maintaining a system of mandatory schooling. After all, they depend on the existence of the school for the maintenance of their position within a complex network of institutional structures that provides them with their financial subsistence." As suggested in Chapter Three, however, the roots of the messianic principle that governs educational discourse runs very deep in the history of Western culture, deep enough to make the crass economic argument subordinate to the historico-cultural argument.

It was also described in Chapter Three how the dispersion of the pastoral power of the church that occurred with the dissolution of the church's dominance as an institution in Western societies has been appropriated by a wide variety of modern institutions. This should not be taken to suggest that pastoral power has been spread evenly across the gamut of modern institutions. Some institutions exert more pastoral power than others. Such power happens to have been concentrated in particularly heavy proportions in the school. This has been especially true in the United States.

The first discourses in North America to present a pastoral image of the of were generated as early as the seventeenth century. The earliest of these messianic discourses were produced by the Puritans of the Massachusetts Bay Colony who, believing themselves to be engaged in the process of creating a model society which the rest of the world would later strive to emulate, set out to school their children in accordance with the principles which would produce the type of citizen necessary to make their vision of secular salvation a reality. In 1636, the Puritans established Harvard College to provide their communities with a cadre of leadership in the form of literate ministers and religious-minded civil authorities. They also passed the first colonial legislation dealing with education—the Massachusetts Law of 1642, which reflected a distrust of parents to adequately train their children to demonstrate the religious piety and civil obedience that were requisite to the realization of their ideal society. Although this law did not actually establish mandatory schooling in the Massachusetts Bay Colony, it represents the first manifestation of the sort of messianic discourses that have continued to project a pastoral image of the school throughout the history of American society.

It was not until 1647, however, that the Puritans established mandatory schooling by law. Reflecting the dispersion of the pastoral power once held by the Catholic Church that was discussed in Chapter Three, this law was named the "Old Deluder Satan Law." "It being the chief project of old deluder, Satan, to keep men from the knowledge of the scriptures," the Puritans imbued the school with a form of pastoral power that sought to mold the child's character in a manner that reflected the teachings of the scriptures (Spring, 1986, p.3). Shaping the character of the child in this fashion was viewed as requisite to the maintenance of what was, in the Puritan mind, a just social order. Other New England colonies followed the example set by Massachusetts, while many colonies to the south of New England established their own compulsory education laws.

Though the Constitution makes some reference to either education or schools, many individuals in post-Revolutionary America believed that some system of mandatory schooling was essential to the maintenance of the secular salvation it brought about with the formation of the new republic. Fearful that disparities in economic power would corrupt the practice of democracy, Thomas Jefferson advocated the establishment of compulsory schooling that would "rake from the rubbish" those individuals whose natural talents qualified them for public service. For Jefferson, if there was to be an aristocracy in America, it should be a "natural aristocracy of talent." And, in marking the origins of the discursive practices that were characterized in Chapter Four as meritocratic, Jefferson believed that mandatory schooling would function as what Horace Mann would later describe as the great equalizer of the conditions of men–the balance wheel of the social machinery. Both Jefferson and Mann viewed mandatory schooling as a potential equalizer of the economic inequalities between classes that threatened the stability of the American republic.

Henry J, Perkinson, in *The Imperfect Panacea: American Faith in Education, 1865–1976,* traces the history of the evolution of those discourses that emerged after the Civil War that carried forward this meritocratic idea of schooling as the key to equal economic opportunity. He begins his analy-sis by pointing out that the depression of 1873 caused people to seriously question the extent to which the United States was really the "land of opportunity." Following the depression, which had sparked some major social uprisings among the four-fifths of the working class who were unable to maintain regular employment over the six year period that the depression had lasted, those who controlled the nation's economic wealth saw the danger that could emerge as the result of individuals coming to recognize that there really wasn't as much economic opportunity in the United States as was advertised. The wealthy few began promoting the publication of their own biographies, which presented them as individuals who were born in less-than-admirable socio-economic circumstances, but who, nevertheless, persevered against all odds to "make it to the top."

Such messages were not new to the American public. The children's books of Horatio Alger had presented the same formula for success, as had *McGuffey's Readers.* In all three instances, the mythical version of individual success in America, the "Land of Opportunity," was heavily promoted. Perkinson (1977) points out, however, "the fact of the matter is that most who rose to the top during this period were not self-made men who started out as poor farm boys, but instead, men who had decided advantages in the race to the top" (p. 115). As more and more people came to recognize this, capitalists like Andrew Carnegie were forced to admit that the room at the top was becoming increasingly crowded and harder to reach. Despite the diminished economic opportunities created by the rise of corporatism, Carnegie, in his *Triumphant Democracy,* valorized the material achievements wrought by capitalism and praised the political equality that had fostered them. In his mind, the American school was one of the central bulwarks of that political equality. "Just see," Carnegie exclaimed, "wherever we peer into the first tiny springs of the national life, how this panacea for all the ills of the body politic bubbles forth – education, education, education" (Ibid, p. 122).

Perkinson explains that as the rise of corporatism choked off the individual's capacity to achieve financial independence via the traditional route of entrepreneurship, schooling came to occupy an even more central position within the collective consciousness of America. The corporations began turning with increasing regularity to the colleges to supply them with the human resources that they needed. At the turn of the twentieth century, Perkinson explains:

> the path to success was becoming much more structured. In the preindustrial days of abundant opportunity, a youth had tested himself and proved his merit 'on the job.' Now the testing and proving was to take place before he ever entered the world of work. The schools were to take over this task. The youth who climbed the ladder would thereby prove his ment and be rewarded with the top echelon jobs. (Ibid, p. 126–127).

As mandatory schooling became increasingly central to America's economic life, calls came for more schools and a more structured school system. And, as work in the now industrialized society became more and more specialized, a further demand was created for the schools to reflect a more vocational orientation. This stimulated the formation of a variety of discourses that tied the economic development of the nation to the school. This conceptualization of technological and economic progress as a steady movement toward increased secular salvation must be recognized as distinct from discourses that tie the economic well-being of the individual to the school. They are two disparate conceptualizations of secular salvation. In the former, the school assumes the pastoral role of selecting which individuals should fill which positions within the economy in order to advance the overall economic and technological development of the nation. In the latter, the school assumes the pastoral role of providing everyone with the same opportunity to achieve economic wealth on the basis of their displayed merit.

In the 1950s, emphasis was placed on the former. Discourses emerged which accentuated the school's function as a sorting mechanism. The Soviet Union's successful launch of Sputnik provoked an increased concern for the school's role as the source of trained manpower. Educators during this period focused their attentions on establishing "quality programs in the vital subject areas [mathematics, science, and foreign languages], inaugurating special programs for the gifted, and initiating comprehensive programs of [career] guidance and counseling" (Ibid, p. 153). The motivation behind this emphasis was for the United States to develop the means to create the requisite manpower to maintain and extend the technological and economic world dominance that it had achieved after the Second World War. The political significance of these events will be discussed later.

Though the messianic promise that the school could ensure that the United States would continue to prosper as the world's dominant power was not completely displaced during the 1960s, this decade witnessed a renewed interest in the pastoral image of the school as an equalizer of the economic disparities that existed across social classes. While the sorting function of the school would provide the nation with a reserve of well-trained and well-paid individuals who could sustain the nation's world dominance, it did not guarantee that people from the lower classes would have an equal chance to enter these highly prized professions. In fact:

> Since most educators and educated laymen during the sixties had conceded that the child's environment largely determined (her/his] school-mindedness…, this meant that in the very act of accepting 'career selection' as the primary function of the schools, Americans had to face the fact that their school system discriminated against what was now called the 'culturally deprived' child. (Ibid, p. 158)

In other words, Americans were forced to realize that, as a sorting mechanism, their system of mandatory schooling was rewarding children of the upper classes for the advantageous situation that they were born into, while punishing children of the poorer classes for the disadvantageous environment that they were born into. This realization, at least on the part of educators, ushered in a set of entirely new messianic discourses echoing those of Jefferson and Mann in their formation of the school as the "great equalizer." These discourses stimulated programs such as Operation Head Start, which strove to eradicate the educational disadvantages of children from the economically disadvantaged classes.

That a high percentage of African-Americans have historically suffered from economic disadvantage gives Perkinson cause to isolate another set of messianic discourses. These discourses have identified schooling as the means by which the racial inequalities that have plagued America can be eradicated. Central among these discourses, and reflective of the conflict between meritocrats and social reconstructionists, are those produced by Booker T. Washington and W.EB. Du Bois. Essentially, Washington brought the meritocratic message to African-Americans, stressing the efficacy of hard work in increasing their wage-earning capacities. In Washington's eyes, education was the means by which the African-American child's character could be shaped so that she/he would recognize the value of labor and the contributions that she/he could make toward lifting not only her/himself toward secular salvation but the entire race, as well. Within Washington's discourse, secular salvation meant gaining the acceptance of whites.

For Du Bois, on the other hand, seeking acceptance was degrading to the African-American. While praising Washington's efforts, Du Bois found them to fall far short of the secular salvation that he envisioned. In order for African-Americans to reach salvation in this world, Du Bois argued that they would have to achieve more than acceptance from whites; they would have to gain full equality with whites. This meant equality in political as well as economic terms. Like Washington, however, he generated a pastoral image of the school. Du Bois believed that higher education was the mechanism by which a "talented tenth" of African-Americans could be created to provide a cadre of intellectuals to lead the struggle against racism and the concomitant quest for full equality.

The pastoral image of the school produced within Du Bois discursive practice is somewhat similar to that generated within Thomas Jefferson's. Both believed that the function of the school was to create a "natural aristocracy of talent." However, while Jefferson conceptualized the function of his "natural aristocracy" as serving to ensure an equitable balance of power within America's political economy, the function of Du Bois' "talented tenth" was to foster dramatic changes within a racist political economy in order to bring about equitable conditions for people of all races.

Jefferson was not the only individual in post-Revolutionary America to make messianic claims for the school in regard to its role in the nation's political economy. As early as 1776, Benjamin Rush had stated that "our schools of learning, by producing one general and uniform system of education, will render the mass of the people more homogeneous, and thereby fit them more easily for uniform and peaceable government" (pp. 758–759). Rush went on in his essay "On the Mode of Education Proper in a Republic" to say that, if we are to be successful in producing Republican machines, we should "let our pupil be taught that he does not belong to himself, but that he is public property" (Ibid, p. 760). While Jefferson wanted to establish a system of mandatory schooling that would provide the republic with a cadre of leadership who would value the principles of democracy and take care to maintain a just society, Rush envisioned mandatory schooling as a system of indoctrination that was to ensure the maintenance of the *status quo*. Toward the middle of the 19th century, though he did not go as far as Rush, Horace Mann envisioned the school serving to inculcate pupils from a variety of backgrounds with common beliefs and values that would ensure social stability and make them good democratic citizens. Each of these figures believed that some degree of secular salvation had already been established with the formation of the new republic. They did not, however, share the same pastoral vision of the school's role in that republic.

That there was no system of mandatory schooling in the United States during the first one hundred years of its history may be partially attributable to the lack of consensus on the role that it should play in the political economy. The potential for abuse was widely recognized. As informal allegiances between wealthy capitalists and politicians contributed toward the increased corruption of the government in the years following the Civil War, a reform party was established among some of the most learned individuals in the country. In the view of these Liberal Republicans, the lack of mandatory schooling had contributed heavily toward the corruption of the government. One of the spokespeople for this group was educator William T. Harris, who charged that:

> All the evils which we suffer politically may be traced to the existence of an immense mass of ignorant, illiterate, or semi-educated people who assist in governing the country while they possess no insight into the true nature of the issues which they attempt to decide. (Perkinson, 1977, p. 171)

For a democratic system of government to meet Harris' standards of secular salvation, its citizens must come to a proper understanding of the underlying rationality of their society. Such an understanding must also be accompanied by an acceptance of the rational authority embedded within the values and ideas that have given shape to the social order. This, of course, assumes a form of intellectual meritocracy similar to that advanced in Plato's *Republic*. Accepting rationality means bowing to the authority of intellectuals like Harris, who would serve as the benevolent philosopher kings of the rational society. Both the understanding of society's underlying rationality and the acceptance of the authority of those who lead in accordance with that rationality are to be developed through a system of obligatory schooling. For Harris, then, the school has a double pastoral image. On the one hand, in bringing the individual to an understanding of society's underlying rationality, the school is projected within Harris' discourse as "the nursery of civilization." On the other hand, in leading the child to accept the authority of the "philosopher kings," Harris's discourse projected the school as "the center of discipline." The school, in carrying out this double function, would, at once, serve to provide citizens with a proper understanding of the issues and platforms that they were to vote on (thus ensuring a "just" society) and provide that society with a high degree of stability by postulating a locus of proper authority.

Another discursive figure associated with the Liberal Republican party was Charles W. Eliot, the President of Harvard University. Eliot's appraisal of the corruption that had infected American politics was different from Harris. For Eliot, "the American failures of government...could be traced to the refusal to employ experts." Eliot's vision of secular salvation rested on a pastoral image of the nation's colleges and universities, which were to serve as the sites where society's experts were to be trained. The elementary and secondary schools were to teach the non-expert, average citizen, whom Eliot deeply distrusted, to accept her/his limitations and to bow to the authority of the expert in matters of significance, especially those concerning the affairs of state. "The democracy must learn," Eliot proclaimed, "in governmental affairs, whether municipal, state, or national, to employ experts and to abide by their decisions" (Ibid).

At the close of the nineteenth century, the American political scene underwent a shift. Rather than run the risk of striking unholy alliances with politicians, many capitalists decided to enter politics themselves. They also sought control of the government in order to stem the tide of a growing Populist movement which threatened to destroy the plutocracy that Jefferson had feared a century earlier. According to Perkinson (1977), the Populist movement failed to gain political power because many voters were afraid that a populist revolution would annihilate the progress and material advances that had bestowed so much prosperity on America since the end of the Civil War. People feared, in other words, that progress and reform were incompatible goals. It was the aim of the progressive movement, which was distinct from the populist movement, to prove such fears ungrounded.

For the progressives, the point was not to dissolve the emergent corporations, but rather to regulate them by expanding governmental control over the private sector. While charging that the plutocrats had tyrannized America with their stranglehold over the democratic system, the progressives were also aware that expanding the size and the power of the government could lead to its own form of tyranny. To fend off such totalitarianism, the progressives argued, the citizens themselves would have to become more active in the political process. For them, a strong democracy was a participatory democracy that shunned the elitist tendencies of the liberal Republicans as much as it did the tyranny of the plutocrats. It was this commitment to participatory democracy that situated a program for mandatory school school at the heart of the progressive agenda.

Since the time of Jefferson, certain discursive practices conceptualized an "educated citizenry" as the linchpin of democratic rule. Progressive discourses differed from those of Benjamin Rush and Horace Mann in that they no longer formulated the function of the school as the "great stabilizer of the American political economy, but rather as its "great liberator":

> A participant democracy needed schools that would release and unlock people, schools that could uncover and help develop the capabilities and talents of every citizen. Once the schools helped the child realize [her/his] own particular talents and abilities, once the school liberated [her/him], then [she/he] could make a more worthy contribution to the political life of the society, enriching the quality of direct democracy. (Perkinson, 1977, p. 187)

In the end, the progressive dream of participant democracy never came to fruition. The plutocrats who had infiltrated the political structure created loopholes in progressive legislation to ensure their own hegemony, while the prosperity and nationalist fervor wrought by the American victory in World War I spawned a certain cultural hedonism and political apathy among the general populace. As a result, while retaining the child-centeredness of its pedagogical approach, progressive educational discourse was stripped of the political and social content that thinkers like John Dewey had originally invested it with.

The onset of the Great Depression forged a new, and more radical, set of discursive practices within the field of education. Many educators associated with the Progressive Education Association were no longer content to have the schools function as a mechanism that would enable society to progress through a series of gradual reforms generated by participant democracy. These conditions gave rise to the social reconstructionists, whose messianic rules of formation were described in Chapter Four. They recognized the Depression as the collapse of the same capitalist system that had previously corrupted the nation's political economy. The function of the school in their eyes was now a transformative one. The American political economy was beyond repair. Nothing short of revolution would bring about the form of secular salvation envisioned by these educators. The discourses of the social reconstructionists, though they have witnessed a revival since the early 1970s, have never gained great currency within larger educational circles. Nevertheless, however marginalized these discourses may be, they are still present and somewhat active within the archive.

Over the past three or four decades, discourses focusing on the needs of the child within her/his social context have been at the center of the archive of educational discourse. The dominant interpretations of this social context have been provided by the meritocrats and their allies who emphasize the school's role in developing human capital to meet the needs of the labor market. Joel Spring (1987) contends that "in the early 1960s one would have been quickly branded a radical for arguing that the United States educational system was geared to meet the demands of international corporate competition" (p. 123). Today, however, few people even flinch as Charles Kurault stands before a yellow school bus parked in some CBS studio on national television and claims that the United States economy demands that the schools churn out better workers.

Adjacent to these discourses within the archive is another series of discourses that also conform to the messianic principle. These discourses have been at work within the archive since the turn of the century, when a vast influx of European immigrants and the migration of many southern African-Americans to the north generated a rapid process of urbanization. Urbanization created a plethora of social ills. Over time, as the ailments of modern life have multiplied dramatically, so too have the messianic discourses which have assigned the school with the tasks of providing American society with salvation from specific evils such as juvenile delinquency, teenage unemployment, vehicular fatalities, drug and alcohol addiction, teenage pregnancies, and, more recently, childhood and adolescent obesity, AIDS and bereavement over death and war. It seems as if the classification of every new social problem or "evil" is accompanied by a discourse which seeks and gains inclusion within the discursive archive of education by identifying the school as the site of resolution, thereby contributing to the escalation of the school's pastoral power.

While the significance of the discourses that have been presented in this conclusion as exemplary manifestations of the messianic principle that governs the archive of educational discourse cannot be overlooked in their individuality, what is most important to recognize is the potential truth in a point raised by Perkinson. He contends that "the American faith in the power of [formal] education has led all of us to make unwarranted, unrealistic, and harmful demands on it" (Perkinson, 1977, p. 121). Similar sentiments are expressed by C.A. Bowers (1967) who claims that the naïve belief among American educational theorists that "education alone could bring into being a more ideal social order or raise the individual to a higher level of moral existence has caused them to expect too much both from themselves and from their calling" (p. 203). Bowers also adds that while, "psychologically, this sense of mission has been both a source of motivation and emotional release [for American educational theorists]..., intellectually, it has acted as a block to vigorous analysis, leaving many proposals to go unchecked by anything except emotional appeal" (Bowers, 1967, p. 203).

It may serve us well, then, to heed the warnings issued by Perkinson and Bowers. Perhaps it would benefit us to recognize the limitations of our cultural tendency to assign so much pastoral power to the schools. Perhaps the schools are incapable of leading us to the secular salvation that we long for. Even if we are not willing to resign our faith in the schools, intellectual rigor would seem to mandate that we, at least, suspend that faith long enough to consider the arguments made by those whose discourses which attempt to make us recognize that such faith is unwarranted. The consideration of these arguments is not possible, however, as long as the forces of exclusion generated by the zealots of mandatory schooling strive to silence them.

Other Transgressions, Other Exclusions

As promised in the opening paragraphs of this chapter, there are examples of other subjects whose discursive practices, like Illich's, have violated the messianic principle of discursive inclusion and have subsequently been excluded from the archive. One such writing subject is Everett Reimer. His *School is Dead: Alternatives in Education* (1970) was published in the same year as Illich's *Deschooling Society,* and Reimer's close association with Illich has led to his almost simultaneous exclusion. To silence Illich is to silence Reimer, so interrelated are their discourses.

Four years prior to the appearance of the works of Illich and Reimer, Jerry Farber published an article in the *Los Angeles Free Press* titled "The Student as Nigger." In this article, Farber conceptualizes the student-teacher relationship in elementary, secondary, and post-secondary education as the equivalent of a slave-master relationship. The article generated a great deal of interest among many students at the time, and appeared in a variety of different publications. It also created a great deal of furor. Farber (1971), in the preface of a subsequent book that included the article and other of his essays, describes the efforts that were made to silence "The Student as Nigger":

> Two high school teachers in the Los Angeles area were fired on the spot for reading it to their classes. A Southern California state senator wrote a newspaper editorial attacking it as an almost incredible abuse; the article was subsequently debated in the state legislature's education committee. Campus editors who have reprinted it have routinely been called on the administrative carpet. Frequently schools where 'The Student as Nigger' has appeared have themselves come under attack from the surrounding community. At one college, a parent who had read it became so furious when

> he heard I was scheduled to speak there that he got 5000 names on a (unsuccessful) petition to keep me off campus...Before long the article became a major issue in a state-wide campaign to defeat a higher-education tax levy referendum. Thousands of copies were mailed to voters. Accompanying material urged citizens to vote down the referendum (it squeaked by) in protest and referred to 'The Student as Nigger' as a 'dirty, filthy source of moral poison,' 'degenerate writing,' and 'obscene pornographic smut." (Farber, 1971, pp. 13–14)

According to Farber, it was often difficult for him to discern whether these attacks were specifically directed toward his use of "obscene" language or toward his ideas. To clarify his ideas, he published a book by the same title as the infamous article. In this text it becomes obvious that Farber's discourse represents a more virulent transgression of the archive's messianic principle of inclusion that either Illich's or Reimer's. He challenges the pastoral power of the school by asserting that "if we want our children locked up all day until they're sixteen, let's at least be honest about it and stop trying to pass imprisonment off as education" (Farber, 1971, p. 37). According to Farber, places and reasons to learn are everywhere, and we do not need compulsory schools to force us to learn.

Paul Goodman represents another example of a writing subject whose discursive practice of challenging the viability of compulsory schooling as a means of educating people has been excluded from the archive of educational discourse. Even at the time of writing *Compulsory Mis-Education* (1962), Goodman felt his discourse being silenced:

> It is uncanny. When at a meeting, I offer that perhaps we already have too much formal schooling and that, under present conditions, we get the less education we will get, the others look at me and proceed to discuss how to get more money for the schools and how to upgrade the schools. I realize suddenly that I am confronting a mass superstition. (Goodman, 1962, p. 7)

The "superstition" to which Goodman is referring here is the messianic principle that governs the archive of educational discourse. He even refers to educational administrators, professors, and other licensees with diplomas as "school-monks" who are guided by nothing more than a "sincere" though "blind faith in the school." For Goodman, compulsory schooling is a "universal trap and many people would be better off without it. Though he suggests many alternatives, as do Illich, Reimer, and Farber, his audacity to even challenge the school's pastoral power to lift the individual and society to a higher level of existence has led to his exclusion.

But we need not rely exclusively on the voices that were generated during 1950s, the 1960s, and the early 1970s to locate discursive transgressions of the messianic principle and blasphemies against the pastoral power of the school. We can reach back as far as the 1840s, to Max Stirner's *The False Principle of Our Education* and the 1850s, to John Stuart Mill's *On Liberty* for just two examples of discourses that transgress that principle. Stirner, a German philosopher, begins his piece with the claim that this generation found themselves on the brink of what we refer to today as modernity. The legacies of the past laid like rotting corpses on the battlefield of history. The central task of his generation, as Stirner saw it, was to define itself at this momentous historic juncture. Educators sought to aid them in this task, but the question that Stirner raises challenges their motives. "Do they consciously cultivate our predisposition to become creators [of that self-definition] or do they treat us only as creatures whose nature simply permits training?" (Stirner, 1967, p. 11)

In its formation of a human predisposition to become a "creator," Stirner's discourse involves conceptualizing knowledge as an active process, rather than a material entity to be learned. Within this conceptualization, the individual engages in knowledge as an active participant in a process without end. There is no distinguishable final stage to be achieved, no perfect knowledge to be attained since knowledge is transitory. As one moves continually through the process, knowledge becomes perfect only when it stops being knowledge and becomes a human drive once again (the will)" (Stirner, 1967, p. 20).

It is important to acknowledge an important parallel between Stirner and Illich at this point. Just as knowledge is formed within Stirner's discourse as a process that individuals move through as the result of some human predisposition to create that is driven by human "will," the rules governing Illich's discourse form education as an authentic human value stemming from the authentic human need to learn. The importance of this parallel becomes magnified when considered within the context of the power/knowledge relations embedded within all forms of discourse that are acknowledged by theoretico-activism. Stirner, on the one hand, in conceptualizing knowledge as a process that individuals are driven to engage in by the force of their own will, which emerges from the human predisposition to create, is aware that knowing is a creative endeavor. By fusing the concept of "will" into the process of knowledge, Stirner's discourse anticipates Foucault's more contemporary notion of power/knowledge relations, the idea that power and knowledge are inseparable. On the other hand, Illich, although in a much less explicit manner, in his formation of learning as a basic human need and education as a basic human value, also interjects a notion of human will into the concept of knowing. The human need to learn releases this will as the individual pursues the value of education.

The fundamental difference between Foucault, Stirner, and Illich is that the latter two thinkers have developed a system of ethics around the power/knowledge relations that Foucault identifies within discourse. For them, the power (or "will' in Stirner's case) that is involved in the process of knowledge is the basis of their ethical argument, for this power/will to knowledge/education is that of of the individual, and it is to be given free reign in the creative process. For Stirner, and a similar case could be made for Illich, the "free person" is one who is left unfettered to engage in her/his expression of will. (Although Foucault has stated that "education may well be, as of right, the instrument by which every individual. In a society like our own, can gain access to any kind of discourse," he has never engaged in the practice of constructing a system of ethics.)

Stirner sets his formation of the "free person" in relief against his concept of the "educated person," the person who has been hindered in her/his "will to knowledge" by schools. Schools present knowledge as a material entity to be attained. They imply that knowledge can be engaged in some condition of finality. In Illich's terms, they present knowledge in some commodified form that is intended to induce some previously determined effect in the learner. For Stirner, to conceptualize knowledge and learning in this manner leads to the imposition of unbearable constraints on the human will. It is upon this basis, then, that Stirner denies the pastoral power of the schools, which explains his exclusion from the archive of educational discourse.

John Stuart Mill (1859) makes a very similar argument when claiming that it is "imperative that human beings should be free to form opinions and to express their opinions without reserve" (p. 53). (Rather than spell out the particulars of his discursive practice, as I have done in a truncated fashion with Farber, Goodman, and Stirner, I would prefer to integrate Mill's discourse into this work's closing argument.)

In Defense of Discursive Freedom

There are presently a number of brush fires being lit within the circles of higher education that signal the beginnings of a battle for discursive hegemony within the academy. These fires, which are now threatening to set the academy ablaze were sparked by the appearance of Allan Bloom's work *The Closing of the American Mind: How Higher Education Has Failed Democracy and Impoverished Souls of Today's Students*. In essence, this book represents a counterinsurgent attack from the political right against the discursive forces of the political left that have dislodged traditional (meaning white, male, and repressive) Western ideologies from their position of privilege. It has sparked what amounts to a counter-reformation of an institution previously identified by Illich as one component of "the new Church."

These counter-reformers seek to gain support from the masses by claiming that the values of the hegemonic forces of "political correctness that are currently at the helm of higher education are out of step with the dominant values at work within the larger society. They seek sympathy from those masses by labelling themselves, and therefore the values of those whom they purport to represent, as "politically incorrect." They draw their lines of battle very distinctly, and seem prepared to launch an all-out attack on voices claimed by Russell Jacoby (1987) to have already been marginalized from public discourse to the point of isolation within the narrow confines of academe.

These actions occur at a time when other forces attempt to heal the wounds inflicted on the American psyche by the war in Vietnam. Television shows like *China Beach* and *Major Dad* attempt to relegitimize the military and its involvement in the affairs of the Vietnamese people, while the military seeks to regain the confidence of the American people by launching massive invasions of the tiny island of Grenada and the small American territory of Panama. The recent

Operation Desert Storm was preceded by exaggerated accounts of the strength of Iraqi military. With the end of the Cold War, there seemed to be little reason to continue investing huge amounts of tax dollars on military spending. The war with Iraq not only provided the American ideology of "manifest destiny" with a new enemy, it also provided video-taped evidence of just how wisely the Pentagon had spent American tax dollars on "smart" weapons. The success of these weapons now opens the door for more military spending in order to develop and deploy ever more "brilliant" weapons, weapons that can ensure that even fewer American lives will be lost in the next war than were lost in the war with Iraq.

The lessons of Vietnam have not been lost on the political right. They are well aware that the dissenting voices that called their "benevolent" actions into question emerged most vehemently from the academy. The irony here is that the degree of opposition to Operation Desert Storm on campuses across America did not approach that which was witnessed in the 1960s and 1970s. In fact, a large percentage of college students were supportive of the policies of the Bush Administration. So, in a very real sense, it is puzzling that the political right can legitimately express any concern with the supposed discursive hegemony that they claim the left has achieved within the academy. Perhaps such hegemony has been achieved within certain humanities and social science departments, but the vocational interests of the average college student that cause her/him to avoid such departments again would deflate the alarm that is being expressed by the political Right.

But my interest in discussing these phenomena within the context of this project is not merely grounded in my personal concern that we may be witnessing the beginnings of a new era of McCarthyism on campus. My deeper concern is with the conceptualization of the academy, and the primary and secondary schools for that matter, as a discursive battlefield where ideological battles are won and lost. The political left has often been as guilty as the political right for such conceptualizations. Therefore, even though I align myself ideologically with the political left, the following comments are non-partisan within the context of the politically correct/incorrect debate.

That those on either side of the political fence should conceptualize the academy or any other school as a discursive battlefield attests to the continued "validity" of John Stuart Mill's (1859) observation that "in our times, from the highest class of society down to the lowest, everyone lives under the eye of a hostile and dreaded censorship" (p. 58). Earlier I stated that I agree with Foucault's belief that education may well be, as of right now, the instrument by which every individual, in a society like our own, can gain access to any kind of discourse." Conceptualizing any school as a discursive battlefield runs against the very grain of this belief. Such practices admit to seeking to censure and censor their discursive enemies. And, the messianic principle of education whole-heartedly promotes this tendency by imbuing the school with a pastoral power that seeks to advance either society and/or the individual to one or another vision of secular salvation.

As long as the messianic principle dominates the archive of educational discourse, our institutions of education will continue to be conceptualized as battlefields, since there will likely never be any lasting agreement reached on what constitutes a "politically correct" vision of secular salvation. Furthermore, these institutions, no matter which set of discourses has hegemony over them at any given point in time, will continue to display their homogenizing effects recognized by Mill (1859), who suggests that the establishment of mandatory education represents an organized attempt to impose the "tyranny of public opinion" on individuals by bringing them "under common influences and [giving them] access to the general stock of facts and sentiments" (p. 70). As long as the messianic principle holds sway over educational discourse, the ideology which informs the public opinion will be subject to change, but the tyranny will remain firmly entrenched within the institutional practice of schooling itself.

Earlier, I stated that this text does not represent an attempt to promote the adoption of Ivan Illich's discourse. While I would welcome the displacement of compulsory schooling by some mass recognition of Stirner's human predisposition to engage in the process of knowledge, I do not envision society being "deschooled" anywhere in the near future. All indications are to the contrary.

At last, the purpose of this project was intended to be pedagogical. In explicating Illich's exclusion from the archive of educational discourse, I have tried to show just how tyrannical the messianic principle that governs the discursive practices within education truly is. The number of exclusionary forces exerted by social reconstructionists, who are largely of a leftist orientation, demonstrates that even the progressive left is not immune from this cultural tendency to imbue the school with pastoral power. So, while I am not arguing that anyone should adopt the discourses transgressing the messianic principle, I am contending that, as educators, we should consciously reject this principle.

What would this rejection mean for us and our pedagogy? Firstly, it would mean that we begin to refrain from using the classroom as a pulpit from which to proselytize our secular religions. In our decision to become teachers, we might question our subconscious desire to have become preachers, to bring the flock into the fold of our vision of truth. Secondly, it would contribute toward the expansion of education's discursive field. No discourse could be excluded as taboo.

I am convinced that the "publish or perish" phenomenon has accelerated the creation of taboos, especially among the left. Professional journals are replete with examples of commentary being used to either marginalize or exclude certain discourses from the archive. As a result, academe has become increasingly competitive, which is a condition repudiated by some individuals who are nevertheless forced to compete for tenure and promotions by accumulating "X" number of publications on their vitaes.

Concurrently, this has enforced a certain homogeneity of discourse insofar as current trends in the journals that publish educational research and scholarship dictate what is "of interest" and what is not. It has also created a system of celebrity. Those who push research toward a new trend are afforded star status, leaving those discourses which are not "en vogue" to be silenced or merely unheard.

In advocating for the rejection of the messianic principle, then, I am in firm agreement with Mill when he states that "if the teachers of [humanity] are to be cognizant of all that they ought to know, everything must be free to be written and published without restraint" (Ibid, p. 37). This applies to the discourses of writing subjects like Allan Bloom as much as it does to Ivan Illich. It also applies to what is spoken within the classroom. But here, an important qualification is in order.

In terms of classroom pedagogy, the dissolution of the power exerted by the messianic principle presents us with two problems. First, if everything is now capable of being spoken within the classroom, how do we go about deciding which discourses to introduce students to? This is, by far, the most difficult question to address. The only viable answer lies in arguing for introducing them to the number and variety of discourses that time allows, not the most "politically correct" from any perspective.

Second, how do we go about presenting this variety of discourses?

Previously, I stated that rejecting the messianic principle involves denouncing the classroom as a pulpit from which to proselytize our secular religions. Thus, proper pedagogical practices rely on the integrity of the teacher. Their personal ideological commitments must be kept in check. As far as a teaching methodology is concerned, I would strongly encourage the development of a pedagogy that is grounded in theoretico-activism. This would enable the teacher to maintain an acceptable distance from the discourses to be analyzed/ taught. A theoretico-active pedagogy would entail an explication of the power/ knowledge relations embedded within the various discourses to be introduced and would entail the discussion of the possible unities and discontinuities that exist between them. Most importantly, while acknowledging that a theoretico-active approach would amount to providing the student with only one possible interpretation of those discourses, this approach does possess the advantage of allowing the student to decide for her/himself which from among those discourses presented are worth further personal consideration. In this regard, the further development of a theoretico-active pedagogy may well contribute toward a method by which educators can avoid imbuing themselves and, therefore, the school with pastoral power.

References

Farber, J. (1986). *The student as nigger.* New York, NY: Pocket Books.

Goodman, P. (1962). *Compulsory mis-education.* New York, NY: Vintage Books.

Jacoby, R. (1962). *The last intellectuals: American culture wars in the age of academe.* New York, NY: Basic Books.

Mann, H. (1957). Twelfth annual report to the Massachusetts Boards of Education. In L.A. Cremin (Ed.) *The republic and the school: Horace Mann on the education of free men* (109–133). New York, NY: Teachers College Press.

Mill, J. (1967). *On liberty.* Indianapolis, IN: Hacket Publishing Company.

Perkinson, H. (1977). *The imperfect panacea: American faith in education.* New York, NY: Random House.

Rush, B. (1957). *On the mode of education proper in a republic.* In S. Cohen (Ed.) *Education in the United States: A documentary history* (758–759). New York, NY: Random House.

Spring, J. (1986). *The American school.* New York, NY: Longman Publishing.

Stirner, M. (1967). *The false principle of our education or humanism and realism.* Colorado Springs, CO: Ralph Myles Publisher.

Index

A

Alliance for Progress, 84, 87
anonymity of the writing subject, 20, 21
archive of educational discourse, 17, 21–24, 28, 36–37, 53, 55–56, 62, 69, 71–72, 79, 89, 91–93, 102–103, 105–107, 100
austerity, 51

B

Bowers, C.A., 36, 103

C

Celebration of Awareness, 28-29, 31–32, 37, 76, 85
Centre for Intercultural Documentation (CIDOC), 84, 88
Christian, David, 6
church,
  in Puerto Rico, 29, 77–78, 81, 84–85
  institutional, 28–35, 52, 76, 79, 81–82, 84–87
  Latin American, 84–86
  North American, 29–34, 76–78, 84–87
  conviviality 37, 49, 51–52, 62
  Cuernavaca, Mexico, 3, 84, 88

D

democratic elitism, 58–63, 71, 92
Deschooling Society, 1, 3, 34, 37–38, 40, 42, 48, 51, 104
disciplinary power, 35–36, 104
discourse
  primary discourse, 10–13, 15, 17, 20–23, 27–28, 32–37, 40, 53, 55–57, 60–62, 64–66, 68–72, 78
  secondary discourse/commentary, 10, 13, 10–13, 15, 57, 59–61, 69–72
  rules of formation, 7, 9, 10, 15, 18–19, 21–22, 27–28, 35–37, 61–62, 65–66, 69–71, 75, 102;
discursive formation, 13, 17, 69
  of the church, as object, as subject, 32
  of the church as a convivial institution, 52–53
  of the church as a manipulative institution, 52–53
  of the school as a convivial institution, 49–51
  of the school as a manipulative institution, 37–38, 48–49, 51, 53
  of the student, 48
discursive practices, 7, 10, 12–15, 21–24, 28, 36, 51, 55–56, 60–63, 66–71, 89, 92, 94, 101–102
Du Bois, W.E.B., 98

E
educational discourse
rules of discursive formation, 36, 66, 70–71, 75
transgression of, 23, 66, 71
Eliot, Charles W., 100

F
Farber, Jerry, 104–106, 108, 112
Freire, Paulo, 3
Foucault, Michel, 3, 7, 11–15, 17–18, 20, 23–24, 32, 34–35, 66, 107, 110,
on the author-function, 11–13, 72
on control of discourse, 11–13
on education, 13, 24, 107, 110
on pastoral power 33–36, 66, 110, 112
on the book, 12, 20
on the oeuvre, 20
on theoretico-activism, 21
on power/knowledge relations, 23;

G
Gintis, Herbert, 63, 65, 68
Goodman, Paul, 105–106, 108
Greene, Maxine, 64, 69

H
Harris, William T., 99–100

I
Illich, Ivan
as counter-researcher, 82, 84
as critical functionary, 37, 43, 45–49, 52, 79, 82
as cultural diplomat, 32, 34, 76. 78–79, 87
as cultural revolutionary, 37, 44, 49–50, 52, 83
as writing subject, 11, 13–15, 19–22, 27, 29–32, 34–35, 37–40, 72
on education as authentic human value, 38, 106
on institutionalized values, 38–40, 43, 82
on learning as authentic human need, 50, 107
on the myth of institutionalized values, 39–40
on the myth of the measurement of values, 41
on the myth of prepackaged values, 42–43, 52
on the myth of self-perpetuating progress, 40, 43
Institute for Intercultural Communication, 78, 81

J
Jefferson, Thomas, 94, 97

M
Manners, Robert, 61
Mann, Horace, 94, 97, 99, 101
meritocrats, 57–58, 60–62, 67, 69, 71, 92
messianic principle of discursive inclusion, 7, 36–37, 53, 55–58, 60–63, 65–66, 68, 71, 73, 76, 88–89, 91–93, 103–106, 110–112
transgression of, 23, 66, 71, 89, 91–92

Mill, John Stuart, 106, 108–111
modernized poverty, 40–41, 44, 46, 48, 53

O
oeuvre, 19–22, 27–28, 51, 55

P
pastoral power 33–36, 53, 64, 66, 68, 75, 81, 88–89, 93–94, 103, 106-107, 110, 112
Pearl, Arthur, 63–67
Perkinson, Henry J., 95–96, 99, 101, 103
Piviteau, Didier J., 72
Postman, Neil, 61
progressivism, 101–102, 110
Puerto Rican immigrants, 30–34
Puerto Ricans, 29–33, 76–78
Puerto Rico, 29–33, 76–78, 81, 84–85

R
Reimer, Everett, 104–106
Rosen, Sumner, 68, 72
Rush, Benjamin, 99, 101

S
salvation
    secular, 3, 7, 31, 34–37, 45, 53, 56–57, 59–62, 64, 66–71, 75 88–94, 96, 98–100, 102–103
    spiritual, 31–34, 76
silence beyond words, 80
silence of deep interest, 87
silence of disinterest, 80–81
silence of syntony, 52, 79–81
social reconstructionists, 60–69, 71, 92–93, 98, 102, 110
Spring, Joel, 3, 4, 8, 94, 102
Stanley, Manfred, 57–61
statement, 9, 18–22, 27
Stirner, Max, 106–108, 110

T
Text One (*Celebration of Awareness*), 28-29, 31–32, 37, 76, 85
Text Two (*Deschooling Society*), 34, 37–38, 40, 42, 48, 51, 104
theoretico-activism, 18–21, 23, 25, 52, 78, 84, 107, 112

U
underdevelopment, 40–41, 44, 46, 48, 53, 79, 81–82, 84

About the Author

A FIRST-GENERATION COLLEGE student, David Gabbard completed his doctorate in educational foundations at the University of Cincinnati after spending four years in the U.S. Army. After spending more than 25 years critiquing compulsory schools and contemporary school reform measures, Gabbard is currently inspired by Slavoj Zizek's call for a Positive Universal Project, which he views as an alternative vision of what our species ought to be doing – in place of compulsory schooling – with its capacities for collective learning.